What pastors, educators
about *Give Me Five fo*

"*Give Me Five for Fangs, Feathers, and Faith* is a wonderful, inspirational, and educational book for children. I love the approach using animals, the internet, the library, and scripture. I cannot think of a better book for capturing the imagination and growing spirit of a child. Every home should have this book!'

–Ron Hill, senior pastor,
The Fellowship of San Antonio, TX

"Discover God's creation in a fun and organized manner! You and your children will enjoy reading and re-reading, learning and re-learning about "God's Fangs, Feathers, and Faith." This book can be easily used in a student's home-school curriculum."

–Rich Ronald, Oak Hill's satellite campus minister,
San Antonio, TX.

"What do an elephant's high-tech ears have in common with how God created us to listen to Him? Give Me Five for Fangs, Feathers, and Faith helps children "connect the dots" so they not only learn about God's amazing variety in His creation but how He has uniquely created them for a purpose beyond themselves. Creative, scripture-based, and purposeful, Give Me Five for Fangs, Feathers, and Faith captures a child's heart to love God, talk to God, and care for others."

–Candace Staggs,
Educator

"The fascinating critter stories are a vehicle helping your child discern for themselves the greater love story of God."

–Gloria Smith,
adults and children LPC, LMFT, MA

Give Me Five for Fangs, Feathers, and Faith!

Give Me Five for
Fangs, Feathers, and
Faith!

A Devotional for Tweenagers

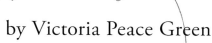

by Victoria Peace Green

(For ages 8 and up)

For Melinda!
The Lord's handprints
are on all He has
created. Can you see?
Psalm 19: 1-4

tate publishing
CHILDREN'S DIVISION

Published by Tate Publishing & Enterprises, LLC
127 E. Trade Center Terrace | Mustang, Oklahoma 73064 USA
1.888.361.9473 | www.tatepublishing.com

Tate Publishing is committed to excellence in the publishing industry. The company reflects the philosophy established by the founders, based on Psalm 68:11,
"The Lord gave the word and great was the company of those who published it."

Book design copyright © 2012 by Tate Publishing, LLC. All rights reserved.
Cover and interior design by Elizabeth M. Hawkins
Illustrations by Kael Little & Kathy Hoyt

Published in the United States of America

ISBN: 978-1-61862-691-2
1. Juvenile Nonfiction / Religious / Christian / Science & Nature
2. Juvenile Nonfiction / Religious / Christian / Devotional & Prayer
12.08.06

Dedication

To Kaelan Lamar and Claire Peace:
I love you both "so, so much!"
When I am with you, our ages are the same! You both
are tucked deep inside my heart forever.
I want to share all that Jesus has shown me with you!

What a large number of things you
You have made, O Lord!
You made them all by wisdom.
The earth is filled with your creatures.
Psalm 104:24 GWT

Acknowledgments

To Jesus, my Savior and Lord, for you are my purpose
in this work. Your Spirit spoke and I wrote.
I love you like none other.

To Thomas, my precious husband, my greatest cheerleader.
Your love sustains me, your daily
encouragement kept *Give Me Five for Fangs, Feather's
and Faith* on track. Thank you, Love, for all your
inspiration and unconditional love! I'll love you forever!

To Candy Staggs, my dear friend and sister in Christ.
My enduring supporter, editor, encourager, and
guide. *Give Me Five for Fangs, Feathers, and
Faith* is a reality because of you!

To Heidi Peace Byrd and Matthew Thomas Green,
my children who are gifts from God.
Your forever love, patience, and encouraging words
encouraged me each day as *Give Me Five for Fangs, Feathers,
and Faith* was coming to be a reality! You are "the best"
and I "love you more than numbers can go!"

How to Get the Most out of
Give Me Five for Fangs, Feathers, and Faith!

Direct your children onto the right path, and
when they are older, they will not leave it.
Proverbs 22:6, NLT

Give Me Five for Fangs, Feathers, and Faith is a fifty-two-week nature and animal devotional created to help your tweenager discover God. As I began to pray about how best to capture a tweenager's (ages 8 and up) interest, God reminded me of what I so immensely enjoyed as a child and still enjoy to this day: animals and all the curious things of nature. Spending time in nature often made boring days as a child explode into days of discovery.

Give Me Five for Fangs, Feathers, and Faith is a devotional intended to excite even the most reading-challenged youth. Your tweenager can begin at any one of the fifty-two themes. Each devotional is planned around the five week days to free up the weekend for your family's participation at your place of worship. Having written children's Christian non-fiction for fifteen years, I found that sharing God through His creation of critters and nature is a sure way to help kids focus. Whether in solitude or with you, your child looks forward to discovering more of God's miraculous design of life.

On the first page of *Give Me Five for Fangs, Feathers, and Faith* is day One, where your tween reads about one of God's critters or creation. They'll also read the *What About You* section which parallels the article. This section helps your tween grow to begin experiencing the love of God. The Holy Spirit begins to grow your tweenager's interest in God and reveal how God is involved in their personal life. I chose each scripture to reinforce both the *What about You* segment as well as introduce your child to how God's living Word can be applied to their everyday life. The New Living Translation (NLT), the New Century Version (NCV), and the God's Word (GWT) translation, are my choices because they are easily understood by any age child. Looking up each verse in their Bible and underlining it emphasizes how God's Word is to be a constant companion. To help your tween easily navigate the scriptures, there is a list of the sixty-six books of the Bible.

Days Two, Three, Four, and Five build on the theme from Day One and are to be read in order. A place is provided for your tween to jot down their thoughts after reading from each day's study. On Day Two, *Check It Out,* your tween is encouraged to discover for themselves, with your permission, additional information about the first days reading, online, at the library, or around your home. God, who made the heavens and the earth and all that "crawls upon it," draws your child to Himself week in and week out through this segment. God is in all that is big as well as the microscopic details that He planned so man would be without excuse to find Him!

Day Three, *Check Within,* will help your tween come to understand they were made to have a personal relationship with God through His one and only Son, Jesus Christ. Further Bible study brings understanding of who Jesus Christ is, how He came to bring saving grace, and what is needed to receive the gift of God.

On Day Four, *Check Around* begins to develop a compassion and tender heart in your tweenager toward friends and family. Once your tween chooses to receive Jesus's grace by faith, this segment begins to bring awareness of and the desire to be the hands and feet of their Savior, Jesus Christ. Your tweenager is asked questions like: How might you be a friend to someone that no else likes? How can I be a kid that can help others be their best?

Finally, on Day Five, *Check With the Lord* is all about prayer. "The prayer of a righteous man availeth much" (James 5:16, KJV). Prayer is the doorway into God's heart. Throughout *Give Me Five for Fangs, Feather's, and Faith,* your tweenager learns to pray to God by reading a prayer as well as writing their own short prayer. On other weeks they will read a Psalm before they pray. Through Bible reading and the working of the Holy Spirit, they begin to experience how prayer connects them as one with God. It is *my* prayer that through *Give Me Five for Fangs, Feathers, and Faith,* your tween will uncover God's tender, unconditional love and mercy.

Learn the books of the Bible!

Old Testament

Genesis

Exodus

Leviticus

Numbers

Deuteronomy

Joshua

Judges

Ruth

1 Samuel

11 Samuel

1 Kings

11 Kings

1 Chronicles

11 Chronicles

Ezra

Nehemiah

Esther

Job

Psalms

Proverbs

Ecclesiastes

Song of Songs

Isaiah

Jeremiah

Lamentations

Ezekiel

Daniel

Hosea

Joel

Amos

Obadiah

Jonah

Micah

Nahum

Habakkuk

Zephaniah

Haggai

Zachariah

Malachi

New Testament

Matthew	1 Timothy
Mark	11 Timothy
Luke	Titus
John	Philemon
Acts	Hebrews
Romans	James
1 Corinthians	1 Peter
11 Corinthians	11 Peter
Galatians	1 John
Ephesians	2 John
Philippians	3 John
Colossians	Jude
1 Thessalonians	Revelation
11 Thessalonians	

Table of Contents

Week 1
Tiny but Mighty Fox

What might the grey fox say to the arctic fox if he came to visit the Arctic tundra for a winter's day? How about, "Oh baby, it's cold outside!" The arctic fox has an incredible ability to live where the winters are some of the coldest on earth[1]. When the thermometer reaches 32°F (0°C) outside, water will freeze. Most other mammals, like the grey fox do not have a fur coat that can stand the arctic cold[2]. But the little body of the arctic fox does not begin to get cold until -54°F (-46.66°C) and then it does not begin to shiver until the temperature outside is -94°F (-70°C)! How many degrees below freezing is that?

From the top of its head to the bottom of its furry feet, God gave this fox a coat of thick, bushy, white fur in the wintertime. This tiny predator keeps camouflaged by shedding its fur twice a year which hopefully keeps it from being some critter's lunch. A perfect insulation combo of fat and fluff along with a short and stocky body helps the fox conserve heat.

In search of food, this small mammal journeys farther north than any other land animal. The arctic fox's neighborhood is from 2,100–15,000 immense acres (that's around 8,000,000 to 60,000,000 square meters) of treeless arctic and alpine tundra. The arctic fox hunts for just about anything that its keen eyes, ears, or nose senses. Either by hunting or lying in wait, this hardy mammal eats lemmings, voles, birds, their eggs, remains of caribou or musk ox, baby seals, and anything else that he manages to kill. [3] This great survivor continues to thrive in the severe arctic weather because he is a determined hunter.

What about You?

God gives the arctic fox his senses and determination. When Jesus lives inside you, His Spirit guides, strengthens, and gives you faith each new day. No matter how tough or upsetting your day is, Jesus is tougher and has more wisdom than any human. Giving God charge over all the things in your day is walking by faith.

The plans for each of God's creations are always on His mind. Just like the fox has a place to hide and sleep, your needs are more important than the fox's. Why? Because God loves you like He loves His One and Only Son, Jesus! He always has been, will always be, and He has always known your name! How does that make you feel? Find today's scripture verse in your Bible and underline it.

> O Lord, our Lord how majestic is your name throughout
> the earth! Your glory is sung above the heavens.
> Psalm 8:1 GWT

Day 2: Check It Out

Arctic foxes are the only member of the dog (canid) family that does something twice a year. With your parents' permission, visit the library or go online to find out what this awesome predator does which other canids do not do. They also will follow polar bears around the arctic. Why? What did you find out?

_____

_____

_____

🖐 Day 3: Check Within

The arctic foxes' small fur-covered ears help keep heat from leaving their body so the foxes can have strength and stamina for the important jobs like hunting and raising young. Read Psalm 139: 23–24. What does Psalm 139 want you to ask God to search your heart for? Why does sin offend God?

_____

_____

_____

_____

🖐 Day 4: Check Around

God has given the arctic fox adaptations so it will have a full life. God wants to be useful in all areas of your life, too. Without its adaptations the fox would not survive in the bitter cold. Read Proverbs 3:5–6. When kids and school get really upsetting, and everything looks bad, who does Proverbs say you can trust? What are you *not* to understand?

_____

_____

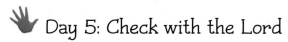 # Day 5: Check with the Lord

Read Psalm 62:11–12 then pray this prayer:

Lord, I do not know what I would do if I only had my own ideas and plans to work for me. You know just what I am made for and how much I can take before I am sad or hurt in my heart. Before I know what is happening, I sometimes believe in what some kid says instead of what Your promises say. Proverbs 3:5–6 is a promise, and it tells me to listen for Your voice in my mind telling me to trust You! Please hold my hand today. In Jesus's name I pray, Amen.

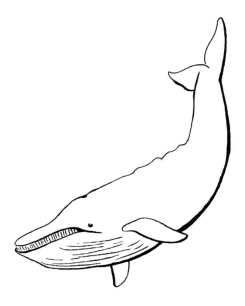

Week 2
A Whale of a Mammal

A fish is a fish is a fish. Maybe so, unless it is a whale. Whales are not fish unless humans are fish. Whales, dolphins, and porpoises all belong to the family of mammals called Cetaceans. Of all the species in the Cetacean family, the blue whale gets the first place prize for being the largest. The blue whale is also the largest *mammal* on earth and always has been[1]. No Tyrannosaurus Rex could have matched the size and power of the largest animal to ever live on earth[2].

The most humongous blue whale that has ever lived was a 110-foot-long, (33.53 meters), south Atlantic, blue whale. Do the math. Does one and a half times as long as an Olympic pool sound right? Weighing in at almost 190 tons (169.64 long tons), this big guy was about the weight of twenty-three male, African elephants[3]. So, with those two numbers, if the average African male elephant weighs 8 tons (7.26 metric tons), about how many elephants equal the weight of the world's largest animal ever? Next time you look at a mid-size car remember a blue whale's heart.

Why? Because it is roughly that large! Its blood vessels are big enough that we could swim through them. Pretty amazing to think about!

The oceans are the blue whales' playground and highway. Instead of legs and arms, whales were created with flippers and powerful tails. Moving through the ocean with their mouth open, blue whales will guzzle thousands of gallons of water filled with krill and plankton. This giant eats some of the tiniest animals on earth. Blue whales are baleen whales. They do not have teeth, but God created a way for the whale to eat. Thousands of tiny plankton and krill are filtered through the whales' baleen. Baleen is a strong, yet bendable material made out of keratin (care-uh-tin), which is the same material that makes up our hair and fingernails. These plates hang from the whale's upper jaw. As much as 8,000 lbs. (3,629 kg) of the super tiny plankton and krill are eaten each day by this mega whale[4].

What about You?

Everything is huge about whales except what they eat. Being the largest animal of the oceans (or anywhere), you would think the whole ocean could be their menu. God gave them baleen instead of teeth, and they are satisfied with the tiny but plentiful plankton and krill—not needy of anything.

Just like the big whale has his own way in the ocean, you can choose your friends, or the places you want to go. Jesus gives Christians the Holy Spirit. He guides you everyday, all day long. The Holy Spirit reminds you of all the things God has taught you. Praising God with your arms raised up to Him is an awesome way to show Him your joy. The Bible says: "He delights over you with singing." Another way to love God is with a song inside your heart. Find today's scripture verses in your Bible and underline them.

And in Christ, God put his special mark of ownership on you by giving you the Holy Spirit that he had promised. That Holy Spirit is the guarantee that we will receive what God promised for his people...
Ephesians 1: 13b, 14a, NCV

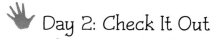

Day 2: Check It Out

Cetacean is the name of a group or order of animals to which whales, dolphins, and porpoises belong. If you were a whale, you would be either a toothed whale or a baleen whale. With your parents' permission, visit the library or go online to find out more about the great blue whale. How many elephants would equal the weight of one blue whale? What did you find out?

_____

_____

_____

Day 3: Check Within

A whale was used by God to bring about His plans long before Christ was born on earth. Before you go to bed tonight, take some time to read the short story of Jonah in your Bible. While Jonah was inside the monstrous whale's belly, he realized that he had been wrong. What is Jonah really saying to God in his prayer? When have you felt like Jonah?

_____

_____

_____

Day 4: Check Around

Jonah was one of God's prophets. That meant he would listen to God and tell others what God told him to tell them. While Jonah was on the ship to Tarshish, he told the sailors something very important. What does Chapter 1:10 say? It says the "sailors became terrified." What might have made them afraid? If you are a Christian, what would have frightened you if you were on board? If you are a Christian, how do others know that you are one?

_____

_____

_____

 ## Day 5: Check with the Lord

Pray this prayer:

Lord God, I am disobedient so many times. Just like Jonah, sometimes I ignore You on purpose and do what I want instead of what the Bible says is right. Why do I have to be like that? I am sorry for that attitude. Just like the blue whale finds tiny krill to be satisfying, I want to be satisfied with all things that You provide me. Teach me, God, to have a gracious attitude when I receive from others. In Jesus's name I pray, Amen.

Write your own short prayer asking God to give you a heart that is satisfied with what you already have and thank Him for what He will do for you.

Week 3
Canada's Dall Sheep

Imagine you are on an adventure in the Canadian backcountry with your friends. High above the jagged cliffs in the Canadian Northwest, you might spy what looks like little bits of salt and pepper through your binoculars. The Canadian Northwest and Alaska have been home to Dall sheep for centuries. Bright, white wool with brownish, backward-curved horns make these guys stand out from other sheep species.

Looking through your binoculars, you would be able to see the world's only white, *wild* sheep. Weighing as much as 110–250 pounds (49.89 - 113.4 kg), the rams and ewes both carry around curved horns made of the same stuff your fingernails are made of—keratin. Fingernails are not heavy, but these mighty, big horns are very heavy. Only during the breeding times do the mature rams (those about seven to nine years old) fight for dominance or who will be "king" over all of the rocky slopes.[2]

High on the steep slopes the sheep rest and feed during the winter months, safe from any predators.[3] Good grazing places can be forty miles apart, yet the older rams know the way to get to the patches of good food! [4] In May and June, the ewes give birth on the most rugged cliffs, which helps keep predators from their lambs. Within a week, the little ones are munching food alongside their moms and dads. [5]

God has created these sure-footed creatures with hooves that guide each footstep on the blustery cliffs. Yet their habitat could bring sure death with a slip of the hoof. The winds sweep the slippery slopes free of snow, allowing the lichens to be easily spotted and eaten. Lichens are the Dall sheep's winter menu[6] But like all prey animals, Dall sheep must keep moving. Climbing around the cliffs all winter long keeps them above their predators. But no matter how high they climb, they will wind their way to the lower cliffs in time for the summer veggies and mineral salt licks[7].

What about You?

No matter where you live on earth, or what sort of life you live, healthy or disabled, the Lord has created you in a unique way. Yep! He planned every part of your life. God knows His sheep (John: 10:27) before they are born. If you are one of Jesus's sheep, take comfort because He knows just what is best for your life.

Each Dall sheep was created by the Lord, and each one was created for the world they live in. Though the alpine ridges seem treacherous to you, God *placed* the sheep on those slopes with all they need to be victorious. You can sing about how strong God is and, in faith, choose to thank Him in all the situations you find yourself. Both the tough as well as the cool because He promises to be with you always. Thank the Lord for teaching you His ways. And thank Him because His ways are greater than yours. Find today's scripture verses in your Bible and underline them.

I look up to the mountains, does my help come from there? My help comes from the Lord, who made heaven and earth! He will not let you stumble; the one who watches over you will not sleep.
Psalm 121:1–3, NLT

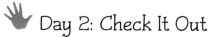

Day 2: Check It Out

Both male and female sheep carry a set of curled horns all year long. With your parents' permission, visit the library or go online to find out about Dall sheep horns. The curly horns grow in summer and stop growing in winter. What are annuli? How do these annuli help us understand how old each sheep might be? What did you find out?

_____

_____

_____

Day 3: Check Within

The mighty Dall sheep's cloven hooves with rough pads help bring safety to their stay on Alaska's slippery and windy slopes. God provides these tools of success for the sheep, and He will also take tender care of you. As you read Isaiah 40:11, think about and then write how God "carried" or comforted you at a time when you felt scared or sad.

_____

_____

_____

Day 4: Check Around

Come springtime, lambs are born on the high cliffs. Both the cliffs and grassy valleys are the sheep's world. The sheep do not worry about danger. But they know danger is always around, so they keep climbing and eating. Read 2 Thessalonians 3:3. Do you have a friend who is always worried about something and when you help calm them down, they find something else to worry about? Trusting God is something we have to practice or something we have to get in the habit of doing. How can you help that friend?

_____

_____

_____

 ## Day 5: Check with the Lord

Read Psalm 63: 6–7 then pray this prayer:

Thank you Jesus because I can lay my head down and know that I am protected. Help me not to worry. Help me instead to trust. Trusting You is giving You all my problems so I do not keep them to myself and worry! When I listen to the Holy Spirit in my quiet time I know He will encourage me to give Him my worries and replace them with His peace. So I will thank You Lord now because I plan to watch how You will change or transform my problems so that they work for my good! In Jesus's name I pray, Amen.

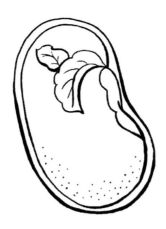

Week 4
Waiting on God

Have you ever wondered what goes on down under the ground? Besides the dirt and bugs, there are seeds with daisies inside, seeds with dandelions inside, and seeds with apple trees just waiting. The baby plant (embryo) is inside the seeds along with the cotyledon which feeds the baby plant. God protects each seed with a coating on the outside. But inside the seed, there are two parts—the embryo and the root of the plant. The baby plant (embryo) inside the seed first needs water then food, so the cotyledon stores this food for later. Some seeds are split into two parts (called dicotyledons) so they have two cotyledons; other seeds only have one part with one cotyledon. Scientists call the seeds with only one part, monocotyledons[1]. When the seed begins to grow, one part of the embryo becomes the plant while the other part becomes the root of the plant[2].

While still in the ground, the baby plant gets all its energy and food from the cotyledon(s). Before they sprout, tiny seeds must have water, air or oxygen, and many need light[3]. No matter how the little seed lies in the ground, once it sprouts, the baby plant will go upward looking for the light, and the roots will go downward. As the seed grows, its roots will find oxygen and minerals from the soil. Water is very important for seeds, but it must be just the right amount[4].

So, what are the seeds waiting for, and why do they wait? They are waiting to burst out of the seed pod and find their way up to the light above the soil. The sunlight is full of energy and at just the right time, God's time, their waiting will be over. The powerful light from the sun and the air will make the new little plant taller and taller and stronger and stronger each new day!

What about You?

Just like the plant seeds, you too were a very tiny seed. But with just the right food, protection within your mother's womb, and the right timing, you were born into this new and exciting world with parents and in some cases brothers and sisters. Psalm 139:13 says, "Oh yes, you shaped me first inside, then out; you formed me in my mother's womb." What words of praise and thanksgiving can you think to say to God who made you and knows each word you say before you say it? What a reason for lifting up your hands and giving God a clap!

God has powerful plans for eternity and for your life each day. But you have to wait sometimes for God to show you the way He wants you to go. Waiting is tough. What is it that you need God to help you wait on? Tell God what's on your mind. Find today's scripture verse in your Bible and underline it.

"I say this because I know what I am planning for you,"
says the Lord. "I have good plans for you, not plans to
hurt you. I will give you hope and a good future."
Jeremiah 29:11 NCV

Day 2: Check It Out

With your parent's permission, visit the library or go online to find out about the plants and trees in your yard or neighborhood. Do you see trees in your yard that lose their leaves or pines? They are called conifers. What do monocots and dicots all have that make them similar? What did you find out?

_____

_____

_____

✋ Day 3: Check Within

Read and think on Psalms 139:15–16. God created you! When you were growing inside your mother, the Lord had every one of your days on earth perfectly planned. How does that make you feel? When you are afraid what should you remember?

_____

_____

_____

✋ Day 4: Check Around

As you read Jeremiah 29:11 on Day 1, you can know God is planning big things for you! What kid or family member seems sad or upset lately? What might you share this week with them to give them hope?

_____

_____

_____

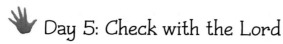 Day 5: Check with the Lord

Pray this prayer:

Lord, You are an awesome God! I thank You now because You made me and love me. I thank You for who I am because even though I mess up and do not always think good stuff, You have great plans for me! You are able to clean up the stuff in my life and turn it to good! I can believe that because Your Word tells me You will never forget Your promises to me. Thank You for all that You made, even the plants and trees and animals. In Jesus's name I pray, Amen.

> Write your own short prayer thanking God for what He has done for you. Ask God to remind you when you are upset that you need Jesus.

Week 5
The Marsupial's Marsupium

America takes pride in its bald eagle, Canada enjoys their Canada geese, and the Chinese adore their panda. When you think about Australia, there are a bunch of critters that might come to mind. Koalas, wombats, platypuses, and kangaroos are only a few of the awesome and unique animals living on the smallest continent in the world, Australia.

Australia is home to most of the world's marsupials. Marsupials are mammals found mainly in Australia, New Guinea, and New Zealand. North America and South America have a few. The coolest thing about marsupials is their pouch. The word marsupial comes from a Latin word marsupium, which means "little bag." All mammals give birth (do not lay eggs) to their young. Most mammals are fully developed inside their mothers, but marsupial moms deliver a baby that is not fully developed. [1]

After the baby is born, it will climb up to the pouch following a pathway in its mother's fur. There it clamps onto a nipple and stays attached. The pouch becomes the life-giving nursery where the baby mammal will grow bigger as it feeds on its mother's milk[2]. Each species has a different rate or time inside its mom before being born and crawling into the pouch. The baby grey kangaroo spends about three hundred days in its mom's pouch. It will climb in and out of its mom's pouch until about eighteen months of age[3]

Kangaroos have upward facing pouches. The Virginia opossum from North America and the wombat of Australia nurture their young in pouches opening toward their tails[4] The Australian mulgara, which is a tiny mouse, has only folds of skin to shelter its baby[5] The pouch of larger mammals, like the kangaroo, is also a great place to hide, sleep, and just be close to mom.

What about You?

The kangaroo joey or the tiny mulgara joey can jump into mom's pouch whenever it is tired, hungry, or afraid. God has made a place for these little joeys so they can grow up safely into what God intended them to be.

On your way to becoming an adult, school, friends, family, and activities are influences in your life. God desires your love and for you to love Him more than all other people and things. He can be like the pouch of a marsupial. How? Jesus will provide the Holy Spirit to be your protector and comforter when you invite Jesus into your heart. Jesus loves you more than you can understand and when life is hard, sad, or painful being a child of the Most High God is the most peaceful comfort you can have. Find today's scripture verse in your Bible and underline it.

He will cover you with his feathers, and under his wings you
will find refuge. His truth is your shield and armor.
Psalm 91: 4 GWT

Day 2: Check It Out

With your parents' permission, visit the library or go online. How many different kinds of marsupials did God create? What did you find out? Draw a few of your favorites. See what you can find out about the smallest and largest marsupials of New Guinea or New Zealand. What did you discover?

🖐 Day 3: Check Within

Read and think on Romans 3:23. Have you wondered why God sent us His only Son, Jesus Christ? Why does the Bible tell us we need a Savior? Read John 3:16–17.

🖐 Day 4: Check Around

Just like the Lord provides a pouch to help the marsupial underdeveloped babies grow stronger, you too can be a help or friend to others. When you see a friend or family member who is hurting or needs help what might you do to help them this week?

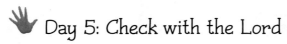 # Day 5: Check with the Lord

Pray this prayer:

Thank You, Lord, for being my protector. You have protected me while I slept, and You keep protecting me from things I do not even know about. Jesus, You want to give me all things that are good for me. Like the joey can jump back into its mom's pouch, I want to know that You will always be my protector and defender. Show me how to be a helper to someone today. There is no place I can go that You are not with me. In Jesus's name I pray. Amen.

Write your own short prayer in your own words thanking Him for being your Protector, day and night. Ask Jesus to keep you safe by listing the ways you want safety.

Week 6
Caribou Need One Another

What large-hoofed mammal gets born and within 24 hours can outrun a human being? And why does this same baby animal need a strong sense of smell and hearing to recognize its mother?

The caribou, or reindeer, of the cold Arctic tundra have their babies in May and June and that baby must be able to run with the protection of the herd within twenty-four hours. When the herd gets moving it is easy for little ones to become separated from their moms, but it's no problem! Their strong sense of smell and super ears will bring them back together. During the birthing season, the gray wolves are smart and will stalk the birthing grounds looking for easy prey—newborn calves that are not quick enough or are sickly are the wolves' focus[1]. Because these deer have a host of hungry predators thinking about them, God always has a protection plan for each and every one He creates. If you had wolves and bears as enemies, how would you escape? God has the answer! How about running? The long-legged caribou can reach speeds up to 50 miles (80.47 km) per hour[2].

On a caribou's menu are plants, like leaves, twigs, moss, and lichen. Because the plants come and go as the seasons, these mammals are known to migrate one of the most difficult treks of any other walking land animal.[3] Thousands of these strong and sturdy deer complete a year-round migration trek of over 3,100 miles (5,000 km).[4] How many miles can you run without stopping? What's the longest trip you've been on?

What about You?

Caribou calves have to be able to run within hours of being born. As a human baby, you could not roll over until you were several weeks old, much less run! Why did God make humans so dependent? Could it be perhaps to let us know how much we need God?

The Bible says the Lord will supply all our needs. God has given you family and friends to enjoy. Just like the caribou need one another, you too need friends. You are also made for friendship with other Christian kids. Be sure to ask God to show you how to be the friend and family member He designed you to be. Find today's scripture verse in your Bible and underline it.

A friend loves you all the time and a brother helps in time of trouble.
Proverbs 17:17 NCV

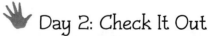 ## Day 2: Check It Out

Caribou can run at speeds of 37–50 mph (60–80 km/h). With your parents' permission, go to the library or go online to the National Geographic website and watch the video for the fastest animal in Africa. What are a few ways the caribou are different than the fastest African critter? What animals are born in the wild that depend on their parent(s) for many months or years? What did you find out?

_____

_____

🖐 Day 3: Check Within

Read Exodus 14:10–14. Like the baby caribou must run with the herd while only hours old, we too are asked to follow God as He shows us. The Israelites tried to serve God the way they wanted and did not obey Him. What were the Israelites to do in Exodus 14:14? What might you ask God to help you with this week?

_____

_____

_____

🖐 Day 4: Check Around

When we belong to God we belong to a very large family—the family of God. Jesus said He will give us all we need because He is so rich in God's love. Maybe this week you could ask the Lord to help you to ask an elderly adult how you might help them. When we are in God's family, we depend on one another. Make a list of a few older people that you can ask if they need your help.

_____

_____

_____

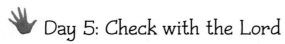 # Day 5: Check with the Lord

Read Psalm 34: 6–7, and then pray this prayer:

Lord Jesus, thank You for the way You take care of everything that You created. Thank You that I can learn from what you created. I can read about how You take care of dependent animals, and that shows me, God, how much You care for my every breath and all my life. Show me how to help those who need my help this week. It is tough for me to do anything without Your help! Thank You for hearing my prayers. In Jesus's name I pray, Amen.

Week 7
Icebergs: God's Life Supports

What could be more cold, lonely, and lifeless than living on an iceberg? Just take a look into your chilly glass of soda next time and imagine living in or around those ice cubes. What good do icebergs have on the earth? Why read about chunks of ice?

Would it surprise you that icebergs are a goldmine to the oceans? The English word iceberg comes from the term *ijsberg* which means "ice mountain."[1] Little mountains of sea ice are like cars for some mammals and can be like baby delivery rooms for others. Polar bears need to get around in the oceans to hunt. Seals and walruses need icebergs to rest. But the seals, walruses, and whales are on the menus of polar bears. Sometimes, the bears will have their babies on or around the icebergs, and other times, the polar bears will swim up to icebergs to grab a snack like a seal or baby walrus. Arctic mammals could not make it without icebergs to feed, rest, and hang out on in small groups[2].

But there is still a little-known fact about the great importance of icebergs. The cold and iciness inside the berg and on top create and keep alive many sorts of almost invisible creatures. Diatoms (single cell algae) are a part of phytoplankton (microscopic creatures) and are among the many animals which are the most important nutrients of the ocean's food web. These seemingly non-visible creations of God live among the nooks and crannies of the icebergs. Antarctic krill (the tiny living things whales eat) live deep in the large caves of icebergs along with different sorts of jellyfish. As the drifting isles of beneficial ice melt, tons and tons of these essential nutrients are let loose into the oceans[3]. All this food helps to create food for larger animals like seabirds and even the whales[4].

What about You?

Icebergs are very important chunks of ice. They serve a big purpose for the larger animals' diets. The tiny creatures living inside the icebergs may seem unimportant. You cannot see them, so what is the big deal? The big deal is that the microscopic nature of these invisible power houses is most important to sustaining ocean life.

Sometimes your feelings seem so tiny or unimportant; you do not want to share how you feel. But your fears, worries, and feelings are very major to God. They are opportunities to bring you closer to the Lord. How? Like the tiny diatoms and krill were created by God to feed larger life, your feelings and fears are understood and seen by Jesus no matter how secret they are. Don't keep secrets from God! He is waiting for you to share all your thoughts. Give God a shout-out because He loved you before you were born! Find today's scripture verse in your Bible and underline it.

The Lord is great and worthy of our praise; no
one can understand how great He is.
Psalm 145:3 NCV

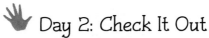 Day 2: Check It Out

If you have a science teacher, ask him/her if they can show you pictures of diatoms/phytoplankton that are found inside icebergs. If not, ask for your parents' permission to visit the library or go online to find out more on those microscopic animals. They are so small, but God uses them to feed what? Draw some of those crazy looking creatures. What can you find out about what a food web is in nature?

_____

_____

_____

Day 3: Check Within

Read and think on John 6:1–14. The crowd was hungry, and the disciples did not know what to do. Jesus always knows what to do. God used something so small like the fish and bread loaves to take care of such a great need as hunger. Do you have anything that is bothering you? What might you tell God? You might see it as small, but God sees it as very important.

_____

_____

_____

Day 4: Check Around

Inside the icebergs are thousands of tiny living animals, but, as discovered in your reading, they are the food that keeps gigantic whales alive! Nothing is too small for God to use in a big way. God is the One who is God, and He lives inside His children's hearts. What can you do today that will show a friend Jesus is always aware of the smallest of concerns?

_____

_____

_____

Day 5: Check with the Lord

Pray this prayer:

Lord, the Bible tells me there is no place I can be that You are not there with me. If You know all about those dinky phytoplankton, You know all about me. You know how I feel right now. You created even smaller parts inside of me than phytoplankton! I know that even the smallest of my concerns will concern You a lot! Let me remember that the next time I get afraid. Teach me to place my fears and daily concerns in Your hands. In Jesus' name I pray, Amen.

Write your own short prayer letting God know with your own words how you need Him everyday.

Week 8
Where Eagles Soar

On the coast of Norway, in the little town of Bodo (Boo-duh), the winters bring stinging winds that keep the waves crashing on the shore. Bodo is known as the sea eagle capital[1]. High in the sky over the streets of Bodo, soar the fourth largest eagles in the world[2]. Sometimes called the "flying barn door," (because their wings are as wide as barn doors), the sea eagle or the white-tailed eagle, makes its nests high on the jagged cliffs that surround Bodo[3]. No other town on God's green earth has as many sea eagles[4].

The sea eagle thinks nothing of the winds and storms that pound Norway in the winter because God created this raptor with all it needs to survive. Long before the storm hits, the eagle will stretch its mighty eight-foot (2.4 m) wings and wing its way up to the lofty cliffs and wait[5]. Why? Why would it not find shelter like the other birds? Other birds hide amongst the bushes in flocks for protection from the coming storm.

What makes an eagle so successful? Unlike other birds, eagles spread their long wings straight out while the winds carry them higher and higher. This monster of a bird of prey is waiting for just the right moment to rise *above* the storm as it approaches. No other bird goes to such heights as eagles do. As the sea eagle soars above the crazy and wild winds, he locks his wings in a fixed position, keeping them very strong as the angry storm goes on down below[6]. Can you imagine flying over a storm? What a view that must be! What do you think the eagle sees at those times and what would he say if he could talk?

What about You?

When things get scary or problems seem to get worse, do you hide, run, try to ignore the problem, or get mad? If you choose to ignore your problems, then you will miss the reason God has *allowed* those problems or fear.

He wants you to *run* to Him for help and answers. Remember how He helped you before (which is your faith) and so you can trust Him again. Then you will come to find that He is the Rock who will protect you. Allow Him to show you how He will take care of the scary thing or hard problem. It is really hard to wait on the Lord and to not act out quickly just because you are uncomfortable. If you are scared or uncomfortable today, ask Him to show you what to do. He will hear and help because He loves you so very much. When you ask, be sure to look for how He will help you. Find today's scripture verse in your Bible and underline it.

The people who trust in the Lord will become strong again.
They will rise up as an eagle in the sky; they will run and
not need rest; they will walk and not become tired.
Isaiah 40:31 NCV

Day 2: Check It Out

Birds of prey or raptors are very different than other birds. With your parents' permission, visit the library, or go online to find out how they are different than other birds. If you can visit your zoo, bring your camera and take some pictures of birds of prey and other birds. Look at how they are different. Hint: It is something about the feet, beak, eyes, and a few other parts of the bird. What did you find out?

_____

_____

_____

🖐 Day 3: Check Within

The eagle climbs above the storm. It does not fight against or become part of the storm. Instead it uses the tools God gave it (wings and strength) to stay above the storm. Read Matthew 14:25–31. Peter began to trust as he walked out on the water, but what happened? What did he begin to do that caused him to sink? What have you doubted God about lately?

_____

_____

_____

🖐 Day 4: Check Around

Doubt crushes our faith. Like the eagle that did not get in the storm but stayed above it, we can stop doubting and trust Jesus with the storms of our everyday life. Like it says in day one's scripture in Isaiah, trusting means that, though we do not see any answers, faith in Jesus's promises gives our mind, body, and spirit strength. What friend or family member needs to be encouraged with the promise of Isaiah 40:31?

_____

_____

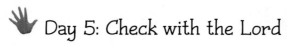 # Day 5: Check with the Lord

Read Psalm 18:16–18 then pray this prayer:

Thank you God for being with me no matter where I go, whether it's to school, to play outside, to hang out with friends, or home. The story of the eagle soaring above the storm helps when I start to doubt or get afraid. I have discovered You are my strength to soar above the hard things that bother me. I want to trust You today inside my heart when the tough stuff makes me want to doubt and be afraid. In Jesus's name I pray, Amen

Week 9
Trees Chill Too!

As the days grow shorter and fall is in the air, many of us want to chill out inside with a good book or play some video games on a Saturday morning. Trees like to chill out too. The trees seem to know when to get ready for winter. How? They begin displaying awesome, colorful leaves on their branches, and many more fall to the ground[1]. Deciduous trees lose their leaves in the fall and winter months. The sunlight does not get to the leaves as it does in summer[2]. The water, heat, and minerals are not as plentiful as they were in spring and summer. Chlorophyll is what gives the leaves their green color. Two-thirds of a leaf's green is from a sort of food factory in the chlorophyll. When the tree stops making food, the chlorophyll also stops and the leaf does not get the food it had in summer. The tree trunk and its branches "chill out" or rest during the fall and winter. They use just a small amount of the nutrients which they picked up from the soil during the hot summer. Soon, all the trees that are deciduous begin to change colors, displaying amazing shades of red, orange, and purple.[3] Thousands of trees on a hillside or a valley are an awesome work of art by God.

Now, winter wraps its chill around the trees. This stage is called a dormant or sleep state. The trees seem to look very bare because their leaves are buried in the snow. Limited light, dwindling nutrients, and colder weather will keep the plant or tree dormant. Empty branches and lifeless-looking plants make you think they are dead. Looking dead doesn't mean they are dead. In fact, the plant or tree is far from dead. The plant is in survival mode, like hibernation for some animals. Watering or cutting it in mid-winter is not good. That would damage the health of the plant[4].

Only the changing of the season from winter to spring can bring health and new life back into a dormant tree or plant. Be on the lookout in the northern hemisphere around March (in the southern states) or May (in the northern states) for pink and white "popcorn" or blossoms, dressing the trees. Blossoming trees are a sure sign that winter's grip has given way to spring bringing new life!

What about You?

Do you ever find yourself with way too many things to do? Does soccer practice run into dance class and then dance class keeps you from a good grade in math? Do your friends keep asking you to STOP and take some time to just chill?

Resting, like the trees do in winter, is hard for everyone. But if you forget to have some quiet time with God and listen as He speaks through the Bible, suddenly your busyness keeps you away from what really matters. As you sit with your devotion book and Bible, God will grow your heart as you learn to listen for the Holy Spirit to speak to you. Ask God to give you some chill time with your Bible and Him. Find today's scripture verse in your Bible and underline it.

Come to me, all of you who are tired and have
heavy loads, and I will give you rest.
Matthew 11:28 NCV

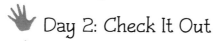

Day 2: Check It Out

With your parents' permission, visit your library or go online to check out the trees where your family takes vacations. Choose two or three of your favorite trees. Which ones lose their leaves? Which ones can grow to be the oldest? What did you find out?

_____

_____

_____

Day 3: Check Within

All around us, nature is busy. What is it busy doing? Read Romans 1:20 and Colossians 1:16. God is totally awesome because He even made nature to show us who He is! He is Creator of all things. No one can ignore God. What does it mean to you when the Bible says "we are without excuse after seeing nature or the things He made?"

_____

_____

_____

Day 4: Check Around

God has given each of us a purpose and a way to live our daily life. Every living thing has a purpose. The flowers give pollen to the bees, and the bees are busy making more bees. What can you do to help your friend that is so busy? How can you (like nature reflects God's majesty) be a reflector of God today?

51

_____

_____

_____

 ## Day 5: Check with the Lord

Pray this prayer:

You are the one and only Creator of all things, Lord God. Thank You, Jesus, for the trees and the animals that take shelter in them. You are the reason for all life, and it is Your plan that trees go through winter, spring, summer, and fall. The tree seems dead for a time, but it wakes up each spring with newness and life. Your creation shows me that You are alive and all powerful. Thank You God that I have arms to lift up to You in worship! In Jesus's name I pray, Amen.

Write your own short prayer asking God to slow your thoughts down so you can be thinking about what you are doing now and not what you are going to do in the next hour or day. How might you ask God for more time to be with family?

Week 10
The Silent Hunter

Imagine standing in below-zero, frozen arctic tundra on a moonless night. Suddenly you feel something whoosh over your head, only when you look up into the gigantic star-swept sky, you can't see anything. Instinctively, you pull your head into your neck. Squinting your eyes, you try to look into the darkness. Oops! There it goes again.

The snowy owl is very protective of its nest. Unlike most owls, the snowy owl is a daylight (diurnal) hunter. No matter if it is the dark of night or the light of day, the snowy owl parents will attack anything they think is a threat to their nest, including people. After the mom chooses the nest site, she scrapes out a bowl shape from the hard ground which is usually on a high spot like the top of a small hill. Building the nest on the ground makes a baby owl a bite of lunch for a predator. These are reasons for both parents to keep a big yellow eye on things. On a pitch-dark arctic night or in the middle of the day, this amazing raptor hears the tiniest move, like the lemmings under the snow or the rabbit moving inside a snow-packed bush[1].

Exploring by flight or lying in wait for long periods, sooner rather than later, the silent hunter will be rewarded. Though God has given owls many powerful traits, its silent wings, lopsided sensitive ears, and extreme eyesight are unique to other birds. Success in this bird of prey's hunt is certain because the owl has huge ear openings (lop-sided on both sides) allowing it to collect sounds whether high in trees or low on the ground. Sight is another tool for the snowy owl. Its eyes can see 180 degrees as it can twist its head in a half circle. This is really a good thing because this silent hunter's eyes are locked in their sockets and unable to move like other birds (or like ours).[2] God has created this snowy owl to be a victorious hunter even in the coldest areas on earth.

What about You?

The snowy owl's unique eyes and powerful ears are tools given by God before its birth. God has also blessed you with gifts, abilities, talents, character, and personality before you were born. When you receive Jesus Christ as your personal Savior, He gives you what the Bible calls spiritual gifts. Maybe you have the gift of wanting to pray for a friend or take care of your friends when they are hurting or sick.

Ask the Lord to show you your God-given gifts. To learn more about spiritual gifts, read 1 Corinthians 12. Remember that each time you use your gift, God will be blessed, and you too will be excited about helping others. God made you and your gifts, talents, and personality to all work together to make you a unique, or one-of-a-kind, person. Remember to thank Jesus, because He gives to us all we will ever need. Find today's scripture in your Bible and underline it.

And God will generously provide all you need. Then you will always have everything you need and plenty left over to share with others.
2 Corinthians 9:8 NLT

Day 2: Check It Out

Owls have exceptional hearing. God made many critters with ears that hear much better than peoples' ears, but the owl has a unique set of ears. With your parents' permission, visit the library or go online to find more about the owls' ears. Look for photos of this amazing raptor's ear openings. How much more powerful are owls' ears than ours? What did you find out?

_____

_____

_____

🖐 Day 3: Check Within

Jesus spoke to His disciples telling them they had ears to hear, but those who were not His followers did not have ears to hear. Read Matthew 13: 11–17. The snowy owl has special ears to hear. If you are a Christian, you too have special ears—spiritual ears that can listen to what God has to say. What does verse 15 say to your heart?

_____

_____

_____

🖐 Day 4: Check Around

Like the snowy owl has powerful tools for hunting food and caring for its young, Jesus has given you ears to hear and "a heart to understand." There are many kids who do not know Jesus but would want to know Him. How might God "tune up" your spiritual ears to be listening to your friends and family member's need for Jesus's salvation?

_____

_____

 # Day 5: Check with the Lord

Read Psalm 42:8 then pray this prayer:

Lord, how amazing is Your love for Your creation. Even the snowy owls are cared for by You. I want to praise You in the morning before I even ask for anything. I want You to control my ears, eyes, feet, and mouth. Take my thoughts and my plans and make them count for You. I want my friends and family to see Your kindness and forgiveness through me. Teach me today to hear my friends with ears like the snowy owl. In Jesus's name I pray, Amen.

Week 11
Lake Vostok

The South Pole is one of the coldest places on earth. The average summer temperature is -56°F. (-48.88°C). Wintertime is not a party either with -112°F (-80°C). The wind chill can make things even more "fun" by lowering the temperatures by another 50°F. (10°C). That temperature of -162°F (-107.77°C) would make life pretty miserable. Antarctica has six months of daylight and six months of darkness. The dark is very dark. One place that is especially dark there and has been for thousands of years is Lake Vostok[1].

Long ago, scientists discovered several sub-glacial (under the glacier), freshwater lakes that are connected by a bunch of rivers! These lakes are thought to be thousands of years old. The largest known of the dark yet pure lakes is Lake Vostok, which is about two-and-a-half miles (4.02 km) underneath rock-solid ice. It is thought to be huge—about the size of Lake Ontario which is one of the five great lakes in North America. Since Lake Vostok is one of the larger of the sub-glacial deep, dark lakes, scientists are very curious about the life forms that may be living in Lake Vostok[2].

Up until 2011, all sorts of technical problems kept them from checking out Lake Vostok. They believe there is possible microscopic life hanging out in the bitter cold and total darkness of Lake Vostok. This belief has had scientists scratching their heads since the 1970s. How can any creature live with no sun and in such bitter cold? In 2011, the drilling began using unique equipment which guards against contaminating the very pure waters and possible microscopic animal life[3]. The scientists were very excited as they anticipated finding life in a place that seems dead.

Adam and Eve were the earth's first explorers as they walked in the Garden of Eden. Lake Vostok is another place to be explored. This is exciting news. Why? It is possible that new life, never seen before or known about, will be discovered. Curiosity is all that is needed to uncover what God has made! God created all things—the earth and all things in the heavens. There is not one thing, not one person, He does not know. The Lord designed deep, dark, cold Lake Vostok, and it is not a surprise to Him.

What about You?

When the scientists began to get ideas about drilling deep down into a place no one had been before up in Antarctica, how do you think many of their buddies might have reacted? Maybe the scientists heard, "You don't need to do that. There isn't anything more to discover" or "Where are you going to get the money to drill?" The Lake Vostok scientists needed encouragement and their buddies to support their plan.

It takes a bold and brave person to go and do what needs to be done. Even when kids make fun or poke jokes at your idea, most of the time it is because they are jealous. They might have wanted to be the one with the awesome new idea. The Bible says in Proverbs that people can have many plans, but God's plans will always succeed. When you have a plan, bring it to God in prayer. Ask Him to give you a bold and brave spirit and for others to want to help you. Find today's scripture verses in your Bible and underline them.

"People can make all kinds of plans. But only the Lord's plans will happen."
Proverbs 19:21 NCV

🖐 Day 2: Check It Out

With your parents' permission take a trip to your library or go online to find out about Antarctica. Draw a small map of it. What animals live there? Who were some of its first explorers? What did you find out?

_____

_____

_____

🖐 Day 3: Check Within

Read 1 John 1:5. Unlike Lake Vostok, which is darker than you can imagine, the Lord Jesus is the Light. He sees all that is inside your heart. Take time now and ask Jesus to show you the stuff inside you that is hard to talk about that makes you scared, mad, shy, or nervous. God knows you and wants you to give all your deep concerns to Him. Read John 10:14. Share some of these concerns with Jesus who already knows what concerns you but wants you to share them with Him.

_____

_____

_____

🖐 Day 4: Check Around

Scientists expect to find pure or pristine water when they drill down to Lake Vostok. Jesus came to earth to make our hearts cleansed or pure. Read 2 Corinthians 5:21. Which of your friends would you share with how Jesus died to take away their sin and is waiting for them to come to Him?

_____

_____

_____

 ## Day 5: Check with the Lord

Pray this prayer:

Thank You, God, for making the world so beautiful. There are so many places and animals that You created or designed, but have yet to be discovered by man. I want to be brave and bold about the things in my life that are good. Your plans will happen no matter what. Show me how to be a part of those plans, God! I need You, Jesus, every day when I wake up. Remind me when I get afraid or mad or sad that You already know about it. Do not let me keep anything hidden from You. I love You. In Jesus's name I pray, Amen

Write your own short prayer letting God know how awesome He is and give two-three reasons why you say so.

Week 12
Butterfly

Have you ever seen someone on TV getting a makeover? They get a different haircut and new clothes, and by the end of the show they look like a completely different person. Their friends and family might not even recognize them!

Every butterfly has the same kind of story to tell. All butterflies have a complete and total makeover. God has plans, and those plans always show what a mighty God He is! The story of the butterfly might as well be called "The Complete Metamorphosis." To become the beautiful insect God intended, butterflies go through a four stage cycle: egg, larva (caterpillar), pupa, and adult butterfly.

Different butterfly species lay uniquely shaped eggs. Butterfly eggs are usually laid on leaves or undersides of leaves. In a few days, the eggs hatch into the caterpillar or larvae stage. The caterpillar begins to eat the leaf it was on, and then it moves off the leaf searching for more food. All the caterpillar does is eat in this second stage, sort of like being at a buffet twenty-four-seven. This buffet-type munching keeps the larva growing, and, as it grows, it sheds its exoskeleton or skin because it does not stretch. Now, ready for the pupa or chrysalis stage, the caterpillar searches for a stem or stalk to hang from. Using silk from within, the creature wraps itself up, and then for a few weeks the miracle of transformation happens in the cocoon (chrysalis). [1] During the last one-two days before emerging, the chrysalis becomes transparent or see-through! If you look carefully you can see its wings wrapped around itself. [2] So then at just the right time, the butterfly comes out of its cocoon with completely different body parts, including wings. The butterfly is a 100-percent different creature. Slowly its wings begin to flap open and shut, allowing blood to bring life into different and strong tissues. Soon, the adult butterfly will look for a leaf to lay her eggs on and the cycle will begin again.[3]

What about You?

Looking from the outside in, the pupa looks quiet and dead-like. But instead of dead, the miracle of metamorphosis is going on. God designed the caterpillar with the butterfly in mind. God sees you from the inside. He knows what you need and who you are going to be when you grow up. That news is the best reason to trust Him.

God designed people to seek or look for Him. Jesus Christ is God's Son. God has given the world the gift of Jesus. But you need to ask Jesus by faith to be your Savior. Then the Lord Jesus will do a total makeover inside your heart. When you pray, asking Jesus to forgive your sins, and believing He is the Son of God who died on the cross for you, He will instantaneously send His Holy Spirit to live within you! At that moment you will be a new creation! See today's scripture. Day by day, year after year, faith by faith, your heart will "morph" to a heart like Jesus's. Find today's scriptures in your Bible and underline them.

This means that anyone who belongs to Christ has become a new person. The old life is gone; a new life has begun!
2 Corinthians 5:17 NLT

The Holy Spirit will teach you everything and will
remind you of everything I have told you.
John 14:26 NLT

 Day 2: Check It Out

The butterflies suddenly go from looking at the world from way down in the dirt to a life of flying, flittering, and dancing on the wind. The first thing they need to do when they crawl out of their cocoon is sit in the sun's rays. What else do they do for so long before they take off? With your parents' permission, visit the library or go online find out more on the butterfly and its wings. What did you discover?

_____

_____

_____

Day 3: Check Within

The butterflies' wings bring them freedom from living in the dirt, from predators that eat them so readily, and freedom to travel quickly. Read John 8:31. What does the scripture say is the way to knowing the truth and being free from all other teachings? How is turning away from sin and asking Jesus in your heart like the caterpillar changing into a butterfly?

_____

_____

_____

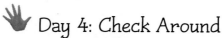

Day 4: Check Around

Though the butterfly is free, can it still get hurt or killed? How? Being a Christian means you are saved and forgiven forever so how does sinning affect your relationship with Jesus? Kids all around say they "love" Jesus, but many of the kids act like they do not. Why?

_____

_____

_____

Day 5: Check with the Lord

Read Psalm 50:10–11, and then pray this prayer:

God, You show me things that many kids do not notice. When I see a caterpillar, I know that someday it will be a new creation. You make old things into brand new things! You take something like a worm and turn it to a beautiful butterfly or grow a brand new leaf in place of one that fell off a tree! I want You to change me beginning with my heart and my attitude. Please let other kids see You in me. Thank You for Your love that sets me free to trust in You and not my fears. In Jesus's name I pray, Amen.

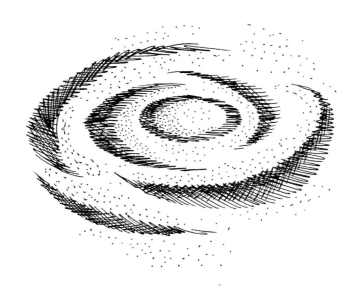

Week 13
The Milky Way-God's Canvas

Our solar system lies inside the Milky Way galaxy[1]. A galaxy is a bunch of stars and interstellar objects floating through the universe and held in place by gravity.[2] If you stand outside on a clear summer's night and look straight up, you will spy a milky-looking line of light. This is the Milky Way galaxy taking up a big part of the ceiling, or directly overhead part of the night sky. What you are seeing is a side view of the Milky Way galaxy[3].

The Milky Way may contain 400 billion stars (give or take 200 billion)! Now that is a lot of neighbors! But as you peer into the Milky Way, only about 2,500 stars can be seen without a telescope at any given time, at any given spot on the earth[4]. Scientists can now see the Milky Way from the outside looking in. They say it is like looking at a long, flat saucer sideways with a bulge in the middle. Our galaxy is only one of fifty galaxies in our tiny part of the universe. Each of these galaxies are pinwheeling or rotating about 360 mps (about 579 kps) around the universe! There are hundreds of billions of galaxies in the universe[5].

A light year is the time it takes a ray of light to travel in one year, or 5.9 trillion miles[6] (9.6 trillion kilometers). The Milky Way is 100,000 light years (LY) in diameter. Do the math. It takes 100,000 years for a ray of light to go from edge to edge of the Milky Way. Given the numbers above, how many miles across is the Milky Way? Numbers like this can hardly be understood by the human brain. So far, science calls the fastest space ship the Voyager 1. As it hurls in space like a giant Frisbee, it is traveling 35,790 mph. (57,600 kph). Imagine if the Voyager 1 kept going at the same speed directly across the Milky Way galaxy. It would take the space craft about eighteen billion years to cross our galaxy![7]

What about You?

Scientists find these planets in their telescopes, but God created them and set them in place! God has no beginning and no end. Everything that exists was created by Him. Something to ponder as you stare into the heavens: no one created God!

Take time tonight to check out the stars. God, who made the billions of gigantic stars, planets, and moons, also made a universe of cells and organs and blood systems inside of you with your name attached. He loves you like His own Son. Jesus came to earth to live, to suffer, to die, and to rise again from the grave, so you could live forever with Him. And all because of His immense love for you! God loves your praises. Whisper a thank you tonight as you look into the sky. Thank God who created you after He created our galaxy. Find today's scripture verses in your Bible and underline them.

Praise the Lord! Praise the Lord from the skies. Praise Him high above the earth. Praise Him, all you angels. Praise Him, all you armies of heaven. Praise Him, sun and moon. Praise Him, all you shining stars… He put them in place forever and ever; He made a law that will never change.
Psalm 148: 1–3, 6 NCV

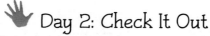 Day 2: Check It Out

The Milky Way galaxy is not alone in our universe. With your parents' permission, visit the library or go online to watch a video about the Andromeda galaxy and the Large Magellanic Cloud galaxy. How many galaxies do scientists estimate are in the universe? What did you find out?

_____

_____

_____

Day 3: Check Within

When you look into the Milky Way, you are looking back into history. How? The light that you see now from one twinkling star continues to come to earth, into the "here and now" even though it may have burned out millions of years ago. Read Matthew 2:2, 7–12. Jesus came to earth over two thousand years ago. As the wise men followed the Bethlehem star, so people today still follow Jesus Christ. Why?

_____

_____

_____

Day 4: Check Around

Have you ever wondered why Jesus was born at night? After all, it is dark, and it is not as easy to get around at night as in the daylight. Read Revelation 22:16. Who does Jesus say He is? Though it is hard to see at night, the light guides us. How can you help your friend or your parent better see *the* Bright Morning Star? Think about it, and then pray about it.

_____

_____

_____

Day 5: Check with the Lord

Pray this prayer:

God, You make me feel special and safe because I know You see me, whether it's day or night. When I think of all the galaxies that bring light to earth I am amazed. Yet You, alone, are the greater Light. I am just one kid in a zillion, but You died and rose again from the dead to bring me forgiveness from my sin. This is too awesome to understand. God, it is a miracle to me, knowing that You are the Light that came down from heaven to bring the Good News who is Jesus Christ, to all men. Help me this week to share Your truth of the Good News with someone who will listen! In Jesus's name I pray, Amen.

Write your own short prayer thinking of something or someone you are very thankful for. How might you also ask the Lord to show you more of His love this week?

Week 14
The Donkey-Jesus's Choice

When we think of Easter animals, we think of cute little yellow chicks, fluffy white lambs, and of course store shelves packed with stuffed bunny rabbits. But one is missing. The Bible talks about another critter not usually set out with the others for table decorations. Open up your Bible and read Luke 19:28–38. Why do you think Jesus chose a donkey to make His entrance into Jerusalem that very first Palm Sunday?

The donkey is both a helpful and tender creature. How? Its very nature makes it helpful. It helps ranchers and their domestic animals. Any fox, coyote, dog, or wolf will be driven from a farmer's sheepfold by a donkey as if it were protecting its own kind. Its funny sounding "hee-haw" will alert the flock when danger is around the corner. The faithful donkey will even lay down with the sheep at nighttime.

Horses have babies or foals. When it is time to wean a foal from its mom, many ranchers will allow a donkey to play and run with both mother and baby for a few weeks before weaning. This is because the donkey has a calming influence over the baby during the process of mother and baby becoming separated. A foal will learn to trust people because it watches the donkey's friendly attitude toward people. Even with adult horses, the donkey is an awesome companion. It helps nervous horses calm down. A horse that is injured or is nervous before a race or recovering from surgery will become less stressed with a steady and calm stall or pasture buddy such as a donkey. These nervous horses look to their humble and chilled-out donkey buddy for support and companionship[1].

What about You

Jesus was expected to come to Jerusalem like an earthly king, perhaps riding on a tall war horse with high-stepping hooves. But Jesus chose the gentle and humble donkey. Remember when Jesus road a donkey before He was born? His mother, Mary, sat on a donkey led by Joseph as they traveled from Galilee into Bethlehem with Jesus inside of her[2].

Every day of Jesus's life, He wanted to show the way to heaven is not by our own ways or by our own strength, but by He who comes in peace. The Old Testament was written thousands of years before Jesus, and it told how Messiah would come riding on a donkey, so Jesus was making that prophecy to become true. But might Jesus's choice be because the donkey's very character reflects the same humble character as Himself? As you read this week look to see how the donkey's nature is like Jesus's. Find today's scripture in your Bible and underline it.

Rejoice greatly, people of Jerusalem! Shout for joy, people of Jerusalem!
Your king is coming to you. He does what is right, and he saves.
He is gentle and riding on a donkey, on the colt of a donkey.
Zechariah 9:9 NCV

Day 2: Check It Out

With your parents' permission, visit the library or go online to: http://www.donkeys.com/inf02.htm. The donkey may be stubborn at times, but what helpful traits can you find about the donkey? Gentleness is one trait both Jesus and the donkey share. What does that mean to you?

Give Me Five for Fangs, Feathers, and Faith!

_____

_____

_____

🖐 Day 3: Check Within

In Bible times, the donkey carried the poor people's things or burdens when they traveled.[3] Read 1 Peter 2:24. Jesus carried our sin to the cross. Think of the worst thing you have ever done. If you have received God's gift of Jesus's grace, then you have also received His forever forgiveness. Read Hebrews 10:17. Today, how can you show God your thankfulness?

_____

_____

_____

🖐 Day 4: Check Around

Like the donkey, Jesus did not get blue ribbons or win popularity contests. Jesus came and still comes with a message of humility, peace, and kindness. Is there a bully in your life that seems to ruin your day at school? How can you change a bad day into a good day for you and that kid?

_____

_____

_____

71

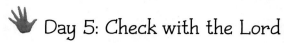 # Day 5: Check with the Lord

Read Psalm 3:5–6, and then pray this prayer:

Lord Jesus, I choose to thank You this Easter, for loving me so much that You died for me, taking all my sin upon Yourself. I will never know the cost of my sin. But I do know that You gave me eternal life with You. Happy Easter! The tomb is empty and You are alive, Jesus, forever! I want to love others like You do. Do not let me ignore kids just because they are shy, not nice, or not cool. Tomorrow at school let me be a kind, gentle, humble, and patient person. In Jesus's name I pray, Amen.

Week 15
House of Shell

Remember the story of the tortoise and hare? The tortoise never stopped for a moment but kept plodding along and eventually won the race against the speedy but prideful hare. Thousands of years and counting is how long this reptile has roamed the earth. He is like a living dinosaur because he lived at the time of the dinosaurs but did not become extinct as they did. [1] What is it that has allowed the tortoise to survive unchanged in a constantly changing world?

The tortoise or turtle is never homeless. Besides being a hiding place in times of a predator attack, its bony shell is a coat of armor. Some shells are as tiny as an inch long and others can be eighty-four inches (213.36 cm)! That is seven feet (2.13 m). This permanent house is attached to the critter's ribs and backbone, making a strong and compact animal. Scutes cover the top of the bony shell and are made of keratin (care-uh-tin) which is the same material as toes and fingernails are made of. Carrying their home around can get to be hot, especially if you are a desert tortoise. No problem, because they use their sharp front claws to dig into the earth and escape the burning sun.

Protecting itself or just at rest, a turtle can hide up inside his shell by crooking its neck into a curve and pulling backward. It pulls in its legs, feet, and tail making the shell a strong fortress. The ornate box turtle, eastern box turtle, Blanding's turtle, and Bell's hingeback are some tortoises which have an actual hinge that closes, fortifying these body parts up inside their shells[2]. Whether the tortoise has used its shell to hide out or to sleep in, the shell has kept this blue-ribbon of a reptile from becoming extinct.

What about You?

With all the hardware God built around the tortoise, you might think the turtle would have a little "I am awesome" attitude. After all, the dinosaurs are dead, but turtles are still alive today. Why not have a big head too? But if it could talk, what might the turtle say? Maybe, "Be gentle, peaceful, and steady, then you will eventually meet your goal." That sounds familiar if you have read the tortoise and hare story.

When Jesus is your Lord and Savior, He gives you the Holy Spirit to teach you peacefulness, humbleness, gentleness, and self control. Give God a shout-out, because He gives you His guidance and confidence to keep doing what is right. Remember to ask Jesus today of ways you can be gentle and steady. Find today's scriptures in your Bible and underline them.

We must focus on Jesus, the source and goal of our faith. He saw joy ahead of Him, so he endured death on the cross and ignored the disgrace it brought him… (3)Think about Jesus who endured opposition from sinners, so that you don't become tired and give up.
Hebrews 12:2a-3 GWT

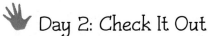 Day 2: Check It Out

If you have not read the "Tortoise and the Hare" story check out the book. With your parents' permission, visit the library or go online to find more information on reptiles? How might their bodies have helped many of them live for thousands of years? What makes them different than mammals? What did you find out?

_____

_____

_____

Day 3: Check Within

Read Ephesians 6:10–18. Armor is very important for surviving in the wild. As Christians we need God's armor everyday so we can be strong over the things that can keep us from being faithful to Jesus. What does the shield of faith mean to you? How do you wear it?

_____

_____

_____

Day 4: Check Around

In yesterday's scripture, verse 15 speaks of the Good News of peace. Putting on the "shoes that share the Good News" gives you God's power to share with others this peace that the world does not know, Christ Jesus. What is the Good News? How might you tell someone the Good News?

_____

_____

_____

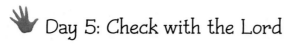

Day 5: Check with the Lord

Pray this prayer:

Jesus, You are like the strong and mighty tortoise shell to me because when I pray, You are working all stuff in my life together for the good. The Bible tells me "You are a strong tower." I can read my Bible, and You comfort me even when I get myself in trouble. Thank You for your invisible power that protects me every single minute. Next time I am angry or feeling upset I will remember to look in my Bible to find a special verse just for me. I want to remember it, God. Sometimes, I forget, so I need Your Holy Spirit to remind me to open up my devotional book and Bible. I love You, God! In Jesus's name I pray, Amen.

Write your own short prayer thanking God for whatever you like, and then ask Him how you could help someone at school tomorrow. He will remind you if you ask Him to.

Week 16
Life Begins in the Egg

The tiniest bird egg is laid by the bumblebee hummingbird. This egg is about the size of a coffee bean (about half an inch long or 1.2 cm) and holds the tiniest baby bird in the world. The largest egg hatched by a bird is the ostrich egg, which is about 7 inches (17.7 cm) long or about as long as a banana. The ostrich's egg is about 4,500 times heavier than the tiniest hummingbird egg. [1] Now that is one hefty egg! An ostrich egg contains the largest single cell on the planet that is presently known[2].

Depending on the animal, their egg shells are made a little differently. Insects and amphibians lay soft-shelled eggs. Most fish have a soft membrane holding all the egg parts together. But some fish have a thick leathery coating to their eggs. Reptile eggs can be hard and leathery or have a soft shell. A bird's egg shell is hardened by the time it is laid, which protects it while the bird sits on it or incubates it[3]. Have you ever taken a chicken egg from your fridge and held it in your hand? It is perfectly designed by God to withstand outside pressure. It is so strong that it is almost impossible to hold it in one hand, squeeze it, and break it[4].

Though the shell is so thin (so the little bird can peck its way out), God made its strength to lie in its shape.

No matter how big, small, hard, or soft the egg is, there is something mysterious, miraculous, and awesome that goes on inside each fertilized egg. God made each of us from just the beginnings of an egg. There is no other way to create or reproduce another animal from the same animal except from their eggs. Each animal begins from a single cell which is a tiny egg, and then, after it is fertilized, the cells inside begin to multiply. The cells slowly form into body parts and the body parts begin to grow and work together. Each egg carries its own power-packed information that will determine exactly what it will be and give it traits that are unique to only that soon-to-be matured egg. This is called DNA[5].

What about You?

From the time you were born until now, you have had billions of little cells growing and changing you from the inside out. There is not one other person like you in the entire world. Like the ostrich egg, your body is strong. Inside your body are soft organs and hard bones. Your heart is the main organ that God created to keep your whole body alive.

In the Bible, in the book of Jeremiah (24:7) God says, "I will give them a heart to know me, I am the Lord." Your heart is soft, because it loves and cares for others. Jesus has a tender heart too. God wants to know you. Have you asked Jesus Christ to forgive your sins and invite Him by faith to come into your heart? Find today's scripture in your Bible and underline it.

> *You will search for me. And when you search for*
> *me with all your heart, you will find me!*
> *Jeremiah 29:13 NCV*

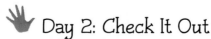 # Day 2: Check It Out

Life begins inside the egg. With your parent's permission visit the library or go online to find out more information on egg gestations for five different critters of your choice. Don't forget to look up in the dictionary what gestation means. What did you discover?

_____

_____

_____

Day 3: Check Within

Have you ever heard the question, "What came first, the chicken or the egg?" The answer is easy, but you need to look only in one book to find the answer. Read in your Bible Genesis 1:20–25. So which came first? Now please re-read 1:22. God blessed the very animals He created. If He blessed animals, in what ways does God bless your life?

_____

_____

_____

Day 4: Check Around

Like the egg has soft insides protected by the *shape* of the egg shell, God has made you to have a tender place inside your heart. Read Psalm 73:26. Who is your strength when your heart may become sad or lonely? How long does it say "God will be with you"? Think of how you can bring that message to your family or friend.

_____

_____

 # Day 5: Check with the Lord

Read Psalm 86:4, and then pray this prayer:

God, when I think about or look at Your creation, I am surprised again and again. I could live to be 120 and still never see enough of Your surprises! Thank You for wrapping your powerful love and protection around me like the eggshell protects the inside of the egg. Thank You for showing me that my strength is not mine, but that Your love inside me gives me a tender heart to powerfully love other people. Psalm 73:26 says "God remains the strength of my heart; He is mine forever." Please let me remember this each new day. In Jesus's name I pray, Amen.

Week 17
The Oyster's Secret

Have you ever been irritated? Irritants are stuff that get in the way of your plans, seem un-cool or bug you. Some days, something that someone said to you can make you mad or sad, and then, the very next day, that kid's same old words can roll off you like rain off a duck's back.

Let's take a look at the oyster living in the deep blue sea. If you could hang out with it for a few months, you might learn how to handle irritating people and things. It has a cool way of dealing with what gets under its skin, or in its case, under its shell.

Oysters are mollusks, which are a part of a bigger group of animals that have no backbones. Oysters are crustaceans that live *inside* their shell, carrying their skeleton on the outside of their bodies[1]. The oyster opens and shuts its shell as it collects food. Often times, a piece of food or gravel will get stuck inside the mantel or the tender part of the oyster. This stuck piece of gravel is the beginnings of an awesome pearl[2]. All oysters are not pearl oysters; the Pteriidae family of oysters create true pearls. [3]

A pearl begins as something not wanted or an irritant imprisoned inside the pearl oyster's shell. When the oyster discovers gravel has become stuck inside itself, it begins to make a substance called nacre. This is a combo of calcium and protein. Nacre wraps itself or coats the piece of stuck stuff. It acts like a soothing substance to the oyster. Day after day, for months and sometimes years, this nacre continues to coat over the gravel or irritant[4]. If you could ask the oyster to open up its shell, you would see the awesome, shiny, and soft glow of a pearl. The pearl is already shiny—no need for polishing.

What about You?

Remember you were going to hang out with the oyster? What did you learn? With the passing of time and with God in your life, the hurts can shine so beautifully. It is true. Just remember the oyster's story—that piece of stuck food or grit which seemed it would be a painful problem became the oyster's treasured purpose.

When you invite Jesus Christ to live inside your heart He is like the nacre. His love is the coating over those ugly words someone said, that rejection from your mom or dad, or that pestering sister who gets on your nerves. Jesus allows those tough irritants in your life because He wants you to see His good come out of them. In His time, God will work those irritants for your good as well, if you are patient. Ask the Lord in faith to do His "nacre coating" over your irritants. He will give you the grace and patience to trust Him. He is just waiting for a chance to turn that irritant into a pearl for you! Find today's scripture verses in your Bible and underline them.

You intended to harm me, but God intended it all for good…
(21) No, don't be afraid. I will continue to take care of you.
Genesis 50: 20a, 21a NLT

Day 2: Check It Out

There is still another living thing that makes its home with oysters. In fact, this animal hangs out with many types of crustaceans. With your parents' permission, visit the library or go online to discover more about the pea crab. How big is a pea crab? Does it hang on the oyster it's lifetime? What is its connection to the oyster? What did you find out?

_____

_____

_____

✋ Day 3: Check Within

When the sand gets stuck in the oyster it does something most of us do not do. Instead of getting mad or quitting, the oyster makes a beautiful thing from an un-cool irritation. Read Philippians 4:4–8. What does this scripture say you should do with an upset attitude? What might you do to keep this upbeat attitude when life gets tough?

_____

_____

_____

✋ Day 4: Check Around

Nacre is pretty cool. How? It soothes all the painful irritation that would otherwise bother such tender parts of the oyster. Coat after coat of nacre covers the grainy and hard irritant. Read John 13: 34–35 and 1 Peter 4:8. Like the nacre covers the gravel, what does scripture say to do with people that rub you the wrong way?

_____

_____

83

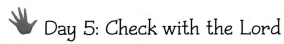 # Day 5: Check with the Lord

Pray this prayer:

Dear God, when my days are busy, and I forget to pray, I know You are with me helping me through that busy day! Thank You for reminding me that, like the pearl in the oyster, I am in the center of Your love. There are kids who irritate me, which makes me have a bad attitude. God, I am sorry because I do not want to walk around with a sad face. I want to bring my attitude to You. God, please give me patience so I can love others even though I do not see things like they see things. Help me to be a friend always. In Jesus's name I pray, Amen.

Write your own short prayer thanking God that He knows your heart. Ask Him to take away anything that bothers you, like a wrong attitude, and replace it with a godly one.

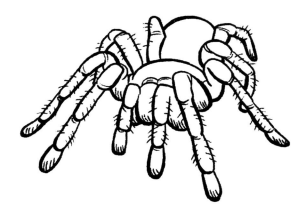

Week 18
Big Harry!

The Goliath, bird-eating tarantula is the world's largest arachnid (Greek word meaning spider). It is one of the spiders who don't weave a web[1]. They hunt for their food by pouncing on it.[2] This mega-spider is the superhero of the spider world, the biggest and strongest spider of all the tarantulas. Its hairy body and one-inch long fangs, make it look like a Halloween nightmare![3] God is big, and He loves to have us discover things we have never seen so we can be amazed at how awesome He is!

The Goliath, bird-eating tarantula lives in the rain forests of South America[4]. This mega-arachnid is about the size of a small dinner plate. Go check out a dinner plate in your kitchen. But when you open up the dark cupboard doors, watch out for mega-arachnids! Even though its name sounds like it eats birds, it uses the same stealth and strength of a cat as it hunts for lizards, bats, rodents, and even poisonous snakes[5]. The Goliath digs a hole or a burrow to sleep and lay its eggs. Even though this critter has eight eyes, its sense of vibration is stronger. It can feel when a possible lunch-munch might come by his burrow and get stuck on the silk[6].

Big Harry is pretty much feared by most animals, except the tarantula hawk wasp. This wasp's bite will paralyze its prey[7]. So this Goliath spider will use the hairs on its legs as darts or just stand up on its legs and make a hissing noise when threatened, making it a scary-looking dude from the wasp's point of view. No doubt about it—the Goliath, bird-eating spider is scary looking, but it is not poisonous to humans[8].

What about You?

If Big Harry could write a book, what might it say? It is the biggest and most feared arachnid and has dart-throwing legs, so it could probably make its book a best seller! But you too have a mega story to tell. God has His big plans for you.

When you invite Jesus to come and live inside you, He will instantly come into your heart and forgive all the sin you have ever done or will do. He takes His heart and places it inside yours giving you all His love! He will do great and mighty things for you and through you. He is a transforming God. His desire is to give you an important job for His kingdom even though you live right now, here on earth. This is one story to tell that is much more powerful than even the Goliath bird-eating spider's book! Find today's scriptures in your Bible and underline them.

I will tell how you do what is right. I will tell about your
salvation all day long, even though it is more than I can
tell. I will come and tell about your powerful works.
Psalm 71:15, 16a NCV

Day 2: Check It Out

With your parents' permission, visit the library or go online to find out about spider webs. If you have a yard, ask your parent to help you look for webs tucked inside of bushes or strung across patio furniture. Take some pictures for yourself. The spider spins silk to make its web.

How does the spider spin a web of silk? There is something so cool about spider silk. What did you find out?

_____

_____

_____

🖐 Day 3: Check Within

Animals in the wild have a strong body, camouflage, wings, or venom because they live with enemies that will hurt them. Read Jeremiah 9:23–24. Strong bodies are not as important as what? Smartness is cool but not as cool as knowing Who?

_____

_____

_____

🖐 Day 4: Check Around

If you could be the biggest kid in your class or school, what would you use your strength for: helping or hurting someone? Read Philippians 1:9–11. What did the apostle Paul want for the Philippian Christians? What does he want for you?

_____

_____

_____

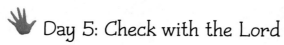 # Day 5: Check with the Lord

Read Psalm 59:1–2, and then pray this prayer:

Dear God, I thank You that You are mightier than any of my problems, more powerful than any of my friends, or any grown up. This makes me feel safe and confident each new day. I don't need to be a bully, use tough language, or say mean things to get what I want. You are growing my character to be like You—gentle, peaceful, kind, patient, and faithful. I need You Jesus, each new day so I can "do what is right and tell about Your powerful works." In Jesus's name I pray, Amen.

Week 19
Tools for Success

Imagine you are sixteen years old and driving an awesome convertible up the highway. Suddenly, way up near the clouds you see this black dot. It dives down and then appears to have stopped in mid-air. Then, gliding on the air currents, the thing climbs higher than you can see. What is this? Finally, you pull off the highway and watch. Is it a jet? Is it E.T. coming to earth?

What looked like E.T. is one of God's exclamation points, the American kestrel. The kestrel is a falcon which is in the falcon family. The American kestrel is the smallest falcon in North America. No matter where you live—suburbs, mountains, farmland plains, deserts, or cities—these intelligent birds live there as well[1].

This bird of prey's body is 100-percent designed for hunting. God has outfitted this small but impressive hunter with powerful body-tools to help it hunt. Check out its well-built 22–24 inch (55.8–60.9 cm) wings[2]. When in hover-mode, its wings beat rapidly. Like a hummingbird or a bee, the kestrel has "one up" on other birds of prey, because it hovers.

Hovering is unique for birds since it is energy draining. The larger the hovering animal, the more energy it puts out to keep its larger body in mid-air. Hovering allows the kestrel's front-facing eyes to see more, giving it greater success in capturing prey[3].

When detecting prey, the kestrel folds its pointy wings and drops lower one or more times before striking. If the prey tries to hide in the grass or bush, the kestrel glides in semicircles before turning into the wind to hover once again[4]. Spying its prey, the kestrel uses the same dropping method again and instantly goes into a 40 mph (64.3 km) dive, surprising its lunch-time meal each time[5].

What about You?

The Lord created the American kestrel and set it in motion. He does the same thing with everyone and thing He creates. God tells us in His word that "All the days ordained for me were written in your book before one of them came to be" (Psalm 139:15b). Have you asked God to show you what your tools are so you can live your life in God's plan? God gives you tools like your mind, body, and talents. How can you help your mind be healthy? How can you help your body be able? And what talents do you have? God is always eager to help you live a full life. Ask Him today to help you!

Find today's scriptures in your Bible and underline them.

I will give thanks, O Lord, with all my heart. I will tell about all the miracles you have done. I will find joy and be glad about you.
Psalm 9:1–2 GWT

Day 2: Check It Out

American kestrels get a "first place" for being the smallest North American falcon. They are not much larger than a big robin. With your parents' permission, visit the library or go online to find more about falcons. What is the largest falcon? Do you have any kestrels in your city? Make a list of the falcon species and draw a picture next to each. What did you find out?

_____

_____

_____

🖐 Day 3: Check Within

Not all attempts to find prey end in victory, or the way the kestrel would like it. Read Acts 12: 5–15. While Peter was in prison, his friends prayed but were surprised when God answered. Can you remember a prayer that you prayed that was answered *differently* than what you wanted? How did God work it out for you?

_____

_____

_____

🖐 Day 4: Check Around

The kestrel focuses on what it can have—prey in front of its two eyes. It is not thinking about tomorrow's prey or yesterdays mistakes. Read Genesis 3:2–6. Because Eve focused on what was not meant for her, she was not thankful for all the other fruit trees God had planned for her to enjoy. What is it that you do not have that distracts you? What things might you have helped your friends do but you missed out on because you were focused on yourself and what you do not have?

_____

_____

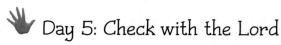

Day 5: Check with the Lord

Pray this prayer:

Good morning, God! I am awake and so glad I have You! Thank You for the air I breathe and the breakfast that I ate this morning. I don't want to leave my house today without praying. My days get all messed up when I forget to pray. Help me, God, to bring You with me into my everyday plans, school work, and down-time. Teach me to hear, see, and feel the simple yet miraculous things You have for me each new day! In Jesus's name I pray, Amen.

Write your own short prayer thanking God for whatever you like, and then ask Him to help you with your anger or jealousy today.

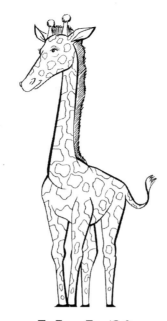

Week 20
Giraffe's Come in One Size-Tall

People have been curious about these long, tall mammals since Noah found room for them on the ark. What are some of the body parts making this big guy a prize winner among African critters for so many thousands of years?

Which neck has more bones, yours or the long-necked mega giraffes? If you answered the giraffe's, you would be wrong. Both you and the giraffe have seven bones in your necks. Each bone (vertebrae) is between ten-twelve inches (25.4 cm-30.4 cm) long and each of your seven neck bones is not even an inch long.[1]

A giraffe's neck bones need to be long and strong since God placed a 500 lb. (226.8 kg) head and neck on the giraffe[2]. Having its brain so far away from its heart, the giraffe might get really dizzy. God had a super plan as he designed a two-foot-long heart with special parts keeping the giraffe's blood circulating and at the right pressure[3].

It takes a long time for a giraffe to stretch out its long, front legs and bring down its heavy head for a drink in an African watering hole. In fact, during those long minutes lionesses or the hyenas would love to munch on the best part of the giraffe—its head. Most of the time, its head is 20 feet (6.1 m) up in the Acacia trees munching on thorns, leaves, and small limbs. Snacking on favorite foods is no problem[4]. The big guy takes a hold of a thorny acacia branch with his rubbery lips then wraps his 20-inch, (50.8-cm), sticky, long tongue around the leaf and pulls. When the branches are eaten up, he takes giant fifteen-foot strides to another tree on his five-feet-long, stilt-like legs.[5]Most other four-legged critters run with their front legs and then their back following the front. The giraffe moves two legs on one side of its body and then the other two on the other side.[6]

What about You?

Long neck, long bones, long tongue, and long legs are all a part of the tallest land animal on our earth today. The more you read about the giraffe, the more you will see how it fits right into the African Savanna way of life. You were created by God and in the image of God. He knew He wanted you to fit into a life with His Son, Jesus Christ and come to be more and more like Him.

How do you become like Jesus? His Holy Spirit will show you how to love the unloving, how to have joy even though stuff is really sad or upsetting, and give you His peace when some plans you have fall apart. He will teach you to be patient during all those times. You can trust Him to be with you, so keep talking to Jesus day by day. Find today's scripture in your Bible and underline it.

You have begun to live a new life, in which you are being made new and are becoming like the One who made you.
Colossians 3:10 NCV

Day 2: Check It Out

Giraffes might look pretty much the same, but they are not. Why? With your parent's permission visit the library or go online to find out more about the giraffe's coat or visit your zoo this Saturday. How many different coat patterns are there? How many giraffes are there at your zoo? What did you find out?

_____

_____

_____

🖐 Day 3: Check Within

Giraffes are comfortable in their quiet and peaceful lives. The only time two giraffes fight is when they both want the same female. Read Philippians 4:6–7. What does the apostle Paul say you should do with things that upset you? What awesome thing will God give to you when you do what he says?

_____

_____

_____

🖐 Day 4: Check Around

A giraffe eats his buffet up in the trees, the rhinos munch on bushes, and zebras eat grasses. Most herbivores live peacefully side by side. Read Genesis 26:16–22. Three times, Isaac and his men tried to keep peace by moving away to dig their wells. Having an argument was not on Isaac's list of things to do. Is there someone you've been fighting with lately? Would you be willing to make peace with a classmate or a family member this week? What plan could you make now to do so?

_____

_____

_____

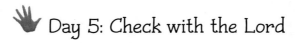 Day 5: Check with the Lord

Read Psalm 53:1, and then pray this prayer:

Lord, Your way is always the right way. I thank You because You show me that my ways can get me nowhere many times. Like the giraffe keeps a peaceful life, I want to show others that I am a kid that wants peace instead of fighting. I depend on Your power and strength to keep me thinking on my Bible verses and to keep me with a good attitude. Help me Jesus, to love and respect others no matter what I feel like. In Jesus's name I pray, Amen.

Week 21
God's Jackhammer

What is black, white, orange, and a little bit red, weighs about one pound (.453 grams) and is about six to twenty-one inches (15–53.3 cm) in length? This critter can chisel a hole into a tree or house twenty times in a second, never gets a headache, and has about a four-inch-long (10.16 cm) tongue. Clue: there are more than 180 different kinds of these all over the world[1].

Well, if you guessed a robotic jackhammer, you might be partially right. Woodpeckers have been known as jackhammer birds. When God made this cool-looking bird, He gave it all it needs to show the world that creation is what God does and not evolution[2]. Woodpeckers have a beak that is separated from its thicker than normal skull by cartilage (sponge-like material) to absorb the shock of the continuous drumming of the beak against the wood. This sponge-like stuff, along with the strong muscles in its jaw, help this jackhammer to keep hammering away eight to twelve thousand times a day! Scientists have said no human has ever invented a shock absorber so great[3].

Woodpeckers secure themselves on a tree or house with their toes.

Each strong foot has two toes up front and two behind. Their tail is like a mini-stool made of strong feathers so the bird sits against the tree in a triangle shape. This shape makes for good support as he drills a hole looking for bugs or making a bigger hole for a nest. His sticky, barbed tongue is coated with glue-like stuff. With a lightning quickness, its 4-inch (10.16 cm) long tongue shoots into the hole, and every little bug inside gets stuck to it. Zap! He has hit the jackpot as he pulls his tongue back into his mouth with no bug stings, and they all go down to his belly[4].

What about You?

Woodpeckers are birds with beaks that never need sharpening, special feet, tail feathers that act like a little stool, shock-absorbing cartilage, and a tongue longer than most birds. After reading about God's jackhammer, can you see a little more of God's awesome imagination? He created this amazing bird from the ground. He placed the woodpecker in just the right habitats around the world. This might seem really hard to understand. But God did not say His creation would need to understand what He created in order to believe in Him.

Do you know that you are way more valuable to God than this beautiful woodpecker? Every time you see an animal, you can praise God for making it and giving you a love for animals. Great is God's love for His creation. Thank Him now. He chose to make you out of the image of Himself. No matter if you do not like how you look or have a disability, Jesus has great and mighty plans for your life and for you each and every day. Find today's scripture verses in your Bible and underline them.

O God you are my God... My lips will praise you because your mercy is better than life itself. So I will thank you as long as I live... My mouth will sing your praise with joyful lips.
Psalm 63:1a, 3–4, 5a GWT

Day 2: Check It Out

The world has about two hundred woodpecker species or kinds of woodpeckers. Red-bellied, Yellow-bellied Sapsucker, Common-Flicker, and Downy Woodpeckers are just a few. With your parents' permission, visit the library or go online to find out which specie(s) of woodpecker you have living in your area or your state. What did you find out?

_____

_____

_____

Day 3: Check Within

The Lord created or formed animals out of the ground. Read Genesis 1:24–27. God made each animal to always be as it is or "according to its kind." A fish cannot become a bird. You are not a bird, or an insect, or a fish. What kind of creation are you? Who were you made in the image of?

_____

_____

_____

Day 4: Check Around

Birds were meant for the air, just like fish live in the waters. God created you to be His friend. Read John 15:15. In this passage Jesus is speaking to His own disciples. Today, many kids do not believe they were meant for God's friendship. They believe the lie that says: "I can be in charge of my own life! God does not care about me." Why do you think kids do not want to be God's friend?

_____

_____

_____

Day 5: Check with the Lord

Pray this prayer:

Lord, I am thankful that I can know the Creator of life. I am amazed when I think about the fact that You made me in your image. Thank You for sending your Son to be Savior of the world. I want to be Your friend just like the disciples were. You're the greatest friend I could have. Please do not let me think or act like kids that do not love You. Thank You for hearing me, God. There is no one who loves me like You. In Jesus's name I pray, Amen.

Write your own short prayer thanking God that
He has given Jesus to the world. Ask God to show
you how you can show Jesus your love today.

Week 22
Living Together-Buddies

Deep down inside the continent of Africa, on an already hot summer's morning, a hippopotamus stands in the shallow waters of a river. Suddenly, a tiny wisp of a bird flutters onto his humongous back. The brave bird begins bobbing its head up and down digging a yummy breakfast of ticks from the hippo's back. Mammals like antelope, zebra, cattle, rhinoceroses, giraffes, and warthogs are just a few animals forever bugged by bugs. The hippo's morning will be a lot less bothersome because of the oxpecker. This little bird chooses its mammal, or meal ticket, and guards it by sticking to it like glue, seldom leaving its "home." Why?

Symbiosis. Sounds like a disease or maybe a misspelled spelling word. Not so! It is a buddy system for many different animal and plant species all over God's animal kingdom. God made this unique and powerful buddy system so that both the oxpecker bird and the large mammal get their needs met. The mammal gets his back de-bugged and kept healthy while the oxpecker bird never goes hungry[1]. Symbiosis happens when

God hooks up totally separate species so they can work together like they're on the same team[2].

Under the deep blue sea, the sea anemone, damsel fish, and clown fish have the same type of symbiotic relationship. Sea anemones are animals living on the sea bed that stay in one place. They are poisonous. If the fish come too close to the anemone, the sea anemones' poison will paralyze them. Clown fish and damsel fish have a symbiotic relationship with this poisonous guy. God created these two fish with a shield of armor protecting their bodies from the poison. They hang out in the "arms" of the poisonous sea anemone for protection. When a larger prey fish darts toward the little clown or damsel fish thinking it will be lunch, the clown or damsel fish quickly darts into the security of the anemone. And zap! The sea anemone poisons and eats the large fish for dinner. There are so many critters with this strange yet cool relationship[3].

What about You?

Our Creator equips all animals with special body parts to help them survive. These parts are like chunks of armor that give them victory in their habitats. Just like the hippo depends on the little bird to rid his sore back of ticks, you also are made to depend on someone. You are not a fish in the sea, but a human in this big and adventurous world!

Do you forget to begin your day with God? He created you, and He knows all about you. You were made to depend on God. Unless you read the Bible daily, it is easy to forget to be quiet with the Lord. Listen and listen again as you read. The Holy Spirit will show you what to read. Go into this day looking for God inside your plans! Will you listen for Him today? Why not thank Jesus now for being with you at every step. Psalm 119:105 says, "Your word is like a lamp for my feet and a light for my path." Find today's scripture verse in your Bible and underline it.

Yes, I am the vine; you are the branches. Those who remain in me, and I in them, will produce much fruit. For apart from me you can do nothing.
John 15:5 NCV

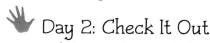

Day 2: Check It Out

God has made a way to bring a union or relationship between living things though they are different species. Symbiotic pairing helps creatures find food, shelter, and safety. With your parents' permission, visit the library or go online to find more about crocodiles. The crocodile has a different sort of *dentist*. What does the croc's symbiotic partner do for its teeth? What did you find out?

_____

_____

_____

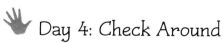

Day 3: Check Within

One thing is for sure, it takes at least two for symbiosis to work. To get the most out of life, the oxpecker bird better know its meal ticket is the hippo. The hippo is waiting for a de-ticking! Read John 14:6–7. Who does Jesus say you need to know so you can know God? Whom does it say has God's love? Read verse 21 now. What does it tell you?

_____

_____

_____

Day 4: Check Around

In their symbiotic relationships, animals depend so much on their partner that in most cases they would die without it. The clown fish would die without the protection of the sea anemone. Read Romans 5:1–2. If you trust Christ through faith, as your Savior, what does the

103

scripture say you will receive? This is good news—really good news. God has someone waiting for you to give this good news to. Who will that be?

_____

_____

_____

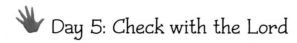 Day 5: Check with the Lord

Read Psalm 59:16, and then pray this prayer:

Thank You, Lord, that You wake me up every morning. I want You to remind me to live for You again today because I am going to need You! I want to act as You would act when I get bugged by a kid or my teacher. Show me how to talk to kids and share the Good News. So many kids are doing their own thing. They do not want to hear anything about You God. Sometimes, they laugh at me because I pray or want to share my faith. Lord, please give me boldness, strength, protection, and, most of all, more love so I can love them. In Jesus's name I pray, Amen

Week 23
Hibernation-God's Great Escape

It is seven o'clock in the morning, and the snow is once again piled nearly two feet high on the driveway on this snowy winter's day. Your brother and you are packing piles of pancakes, syrup, bacon, and juice into your bodies before you tackle the driveway with Dad. Your breakfast is hardy and will supply the calories you need to get through the icy morning.

In winter, many mammals, like the skunks, arctic bats, squirrels, and a host of insects, reptiles, and amphibians are in a safe and quiet state of being called hibernation. Usually, larger mammals do not do a true hibernation, because they will wake up and move around in their dens[1]. True hibernation puts the animal into a coma-like condition that takes quite a bit of time to recover from after they wake up. Limited food sources, cold and frigid weather, and less amounts of sunshine are all reasons for hibernation[2].

Hibernation does not just happen. It is a process. Around September, an animal's instincts will cause them to gorge on food. As soon as the food supplies and temperatures and weather change, the animals' internal, biological clocks tell them to search out and prepare nests, hideaways, and dens—just about any place that will keep them safe from predators and hunkered down from the cold of winter.

Some critters eat all they can find, building up fat which is later used by their bodies as they hibernate. Other mammals that go into a lighter hibernation will begin to store foods in their dens. They will wake up for a few minutes during their hibernation and eat some of the goodies as a snack[3].

During true hibernation, the animal's inborn thermostat will kick in, keeping their body systems (breathing, heartbeat, and digestion) at a stage of constant sleep[4]. Hibernation is God's way of keeping animals alive during extreme conditions. They would freeze or starve to death without God building this great escape from the icy and often deadly winters.

What about You?

Wild animals have to survive a potentially dangerous, foodless, freezing, and icy time of the year. As a Christian, you also face hardships every day. But your Savior and Protector, Jesus Christ, promised to be with you 100 percent of the time. Like hibernation keeps critters hidden from the long freezing winter that surrounds them, Jesus is your hiding place and rock. The tough things that bug you or mess you up do not have to keep you bugged. Pray and give those things to Him. Praise God.

Thank Him because He gives you strength and courage in the middle of all that bothers you. Jesus never sends you alone into a tough place. He always goes ahead of you. Oh, what a faithful God who loves you. The Word of God (the Bible) tells you that, even before you call His name, Jesus hears you. What an awesome Messiah. Find today's scripture verse in your Bible then underline it.

The Lord is the one who is going ahead of you. He will be with you. He will not abandon you or leave you. So don't be afraid or terrified.
Deuteronomy 31:8 GWT

 Day 2: Check It Out

True hibernation is the way animals adapt to low food sources and climate. With your parent's permission, visit the library or go online to see videos on bears hibernating. Then find out online which critters do not go into a deep hibernation. Of those critters, which one would you like to be during a long winter's sleep? Why? Which of those animals do you find most interesting? Why?

Day 3: Check Within

God tenderly cares for certain animals by designing their bodies for hibernation. They are saved from certain death when they hibernate. Read Mark 4:35–41. In this story, the sleeping Jesus made the disciples think He did not care about their problem. What was Jesus trying to teach them? What is He teaching you in this passage about His care and being afraid?

Day 4: Check Around

When an animal is hibernating, it is peaceful and quiet even though the rest of the world is busy above ground. Please re-read Mark 4:39. Jesus spoke right at the storm. What did it do? How many times have you been in the middle of an argument or even afraid in a storm? Jesus lives inside you, and the Bible says He has given you all that is His, even the power to say, "Quiet! Be still." How might you handle the next argument or fear?

_____

_____

_____

 ## Day 5: Check with the Lord

Pray this prayer:

Lord God, thank You that You never sleep. That gives me peace so I can sleep almost as deeply as a hibernating animal. Thank You for saving me from all that could keep me from You. I know You can keep my mind off junk that would harm me and my friends, so I trust myself to You. I can have peace that the world does not understand because You are always available to me when I pray. I praise You with all my heart, my mind, and my body. In Jesus's name I pray, Amen.

Write your own short prayer thanking God for never leaving you alone, and then ask for whatever it is that is on your heart.

Week 24
Cuckoo Catfish

Daycare animal-style is a little bit strange. There are moms who drop their eggs off in other animals' nests and never come back. Some birds, like the cuckoo bird, insects, and even fish species do not have what God gives most moms—a desire to take care of their own babies. Cuckoo catfish use the same trick as the cuckoo bird. Cuckoo birds and cuckoo catfish are known as a type of parasitic or freeloading animal. Parasite fish (and birds) trick the other fish (or birds) into brooding (like a bird sitting on her eggs) their eggs and then caring for them[1].

When a cuckoo catfish is about to have babies, it begins to search by smelling (yes, fish smell under water) for a cichlid that will brood its eggs and babies in their mouths. Cichlids are fish that lay eggs and then scoop them into their mouths. The mom's mouth is like a birds' nest. The little eggs stay inside the moms' mouth until they hatch. The mother cichlid cannot eat during the time she is brooding her eggs. After they hatch, the fry (babies) will come and go into their mother's mouth from time to time[2].

There is something cuckoo about a cuckoo catfish. As soon the cich-lid begins laying or spawning its eggs in a nest, the cuckoo will zoom in and eat some of the cichlids eggs and right away lay her own eggs in the nest. When the cichlid mom scoops up more of her eggs in her mouth to brood them, she does not know she has also scooped up the cuckoo's eggs. The eggs all look the same. And then to add to this craziness, the cuckoo's eggs hatch earlier than the cichlids eggs, so those little fry will begin to eat up all the little cichlids eggs for their first meal[3].

What about You?

The cichlid mom works so hard feeding and tending to what she thinks are her own brood of eggs and then fry, only to end up raising the cuckoo's babies. Like the cichlid mom, you need to be aware of pos-sible wrong stuff that might feed your mind and then your heart. How? The music with mean or hurtful messages, TV shows with violence, or friends that get in trouble, can all eat away at what good God wants to develop inside you. When you receive Jesus Christ by faith, He gives you His Holy Spirit. The Holy Spirit guides you through decisions reminding you of Bible promises, so you can feed good things into your life. Find today's scripture verses in your Bible and underline them.

We pray that you will also have great wisdom and
understanding in spiritual things so that you will live the kind
of life that honors and pleases the Lord in every way.
Colossians 1:9b, 10a NCV

Day 2: Check It Out

Cuckoo catfish have an interesting way of making sure their fry will be born. With your parents' permission, visit the library or go online to find out about Lake Tanganyika. Where is it? How many different kinds or species of cichlid fish inhabit or live in Lake Tanganyika? What did you find out?

🖐 Day 3: Check Within

If you were a catfish, you would think there was nothing wrong with this cuckoo fish! The animal kingdom only wants to make sure its species survive. But in human thinking, this mom seems very selfish and lazy. Read Romans 12:17–20. How should you live each of your days at home and at school?

🖐 Day 4: Check Around

The mom cichlid does not know the difference between her tiny eggs and the parasitic cuckoo catfish's eggs. The only time your mom might get you, your sister, or brother confused is if you have a twin. Mom or Dad calls your brother by your name and then, even though she is looking right at you, calls you your brother's name!

Read 1 Corinthians 13:4–6. What are the evidences in your life (if you are a Christian) that show you to be different than your unbelieving friend?

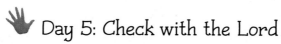# Day 5: Check with the Lord

Read Psalm 66: 18–19, and then pray this prayer:

Dear Lord, You made me to know that I am alive, unlike a fish that has no idea it is living. I know that I am created or made by Your hand in Your image! This is too difficult to understand. Thank You for this amazing animal so I can better understand how You created me. Please know that deep inside, I want to be unselfish which is thinking of others before myself. Jesus, please give me opportunities in my day today, to be giving to others. In Jesus's name I pray, Amen.

Week 25
The Kitten and the Crow

Crows are normally aggressive birds that will attack and mob other birds and small pets. We all have seen cats that attack and kill a bird or sit and wait at the bottom of bird feeders in hopes of a delicious meal. But there is a crow in Massachusetts that might surprise you. A couple found a deserted four-month-old kitten near their home. Little did they know it would become friends with a crow! Right from the time the crow saw the deserted, four-month-old kitten, she never left the kitty's side. Crows normally would tease a helpless kitten, but this crow befriended the little black-and-white kitten. Most crows would take advantage of the homeless little mammal. Not so with this crow. The crow cared for the kitten day after day for many months as if the kitten were her own fledgling.

As the days turned to weeks, the couple called their veterinarian wondering if he had heard of such a thing and what to do. In all his years, he had not heard of this strange relationship and suggested that the couple do a video over the next few months. He knew the crow had a mothering instinct, which is what she might have been using. Each morning, the crow and kitten would walk in the yard together as the crow would pick up seeds and worms and bugs and feed her adopted baby. The crow made sure the kitten was protected by sleeping with her, watching over the kitten while it slept. They played and jumped on one another and teased just like brothers and sisters at play. Protecting the kitten seemed like the natural thing to do each day. If she scampered onto the country road in front of the couple's home, the crow would run out ahead of the kitten making sure it got across the road.

Soon, the couple named the kitten Cassie and invited her into their home during the colder nights. The crow was always waiting for her adopted baby when the front door was opened[1]. The kitten and crow story is a story of hope for runts and for little animals that are rejected or deserted.

What about You?

In this true story, God used the instincts in the mother crow to care for a kitten. Casey was not wanted by her mother or perhaps the mother died and was unable to care for her. But God provided a way to care for Casey that seemed to be wildly strange yet so very awesome.

Does something in your life seem to be almost too hard to do or maybe too difficult for someone to believe? Remember the crow and the kitten. The Lord Jesus is your tender Father and always has just the perfect person or just the right answer to help at just the right time. Jesus knows all about the difficulty. Have you prayed and talked to God about it? Find today's scripture verses in your Bible and underline them.

Love never gives up, never loses faith, is always hopeful, and endures through every circumstance. (8b) But love will last forever.
1 Corinthians 13:7,8b NLT

Day 2: Check It Out

Birds see their world from on high while they fly and from the trees and ground. Their view of the earth is larger than ours because they fly. With your parents' permission, go online and type into a search engine the words "Kitten and the Crow video." What parts did you like best as you watched both animals? Draw some pictures of favorite parts of the story.

Day 3: Check Within

The crow adopted this rejected and defenseless baby kitten. If you are adopted, you can know how special you are because your parents chose you from all other babies. Read Ephesians 1:4–6. The apostle Paul is talking to the Christians of Ephesus. He says God chose and then adopted Christians. There is nothing that can keep you from Jesus except not receiving His forgiveness. What does that mean to you?

Day 4: Check Around

Casey the kitten did not run away from, hide from, spit at, or hiss at the crow. Casey trusted her instincts; her sight and sense of smell told her the crow was safe, and more than that, her care-giver. Read John 14: 1, 17b, 18. Jesus tells us not to be upset or troubled with problems but to trust in Him in our everyday life. What does Jesus say He will not do? Who in your world does not know Jesus?

_____

_____

 ## Day 5: Check with the Lord

Pray this prayer:

Lord, help me to trust You with my fears, the stuff that makes me mad, or the kids that need to hear about You. Sometimes, I get nervous about what to say to them. I really want to make and keep my friends. Please, Jesus, help me to be bold and also patient while You help me with my friends. My faith is from You. Though I cannot see You, I know You are with me. Give me opportunities to talk about You. Open up my friend's heart. Please help me to be forgiving and not hold grudges against kids. In Jesus's name I pray, Amen.

Write your own short prayer asking God how you can be a good friend and for God to open your friend's heart so they will want to hear about Jesus who died for them.

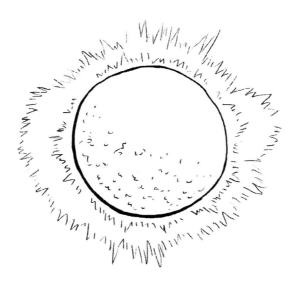

Week 26
Who Is the Center of Your World?

No matter what time of day, no matter what season, no matter where you are on the planet, somewhere, the sun is shining. A forever powerhouse of heat, energy, and light, our sun is our planet's best friend when it comes to all the stars God has created. Why is this true?

All stars give off energy, light, and heat, and many make our sun look like a tiny speck even though our sun is an astronomical 864,000 miles (1,390,473 km) in diameter. But our sun is the closest star to our planet, 93,000,000 miles (149,669,000 km) away. We need it like no other star[1]. If you could jump on a sun ray the millisecond it erupted from the sun, you and the ray of sun would touch down on earth in a little over eight minutes[2]. Think how fast a sunray travels, 186,000 mps (299,337 kps) in one second[3]. The next closest star is named Proxima Centauri. But being 265,000 times further away than our sun, it is not much of a heat source for us earthlings[4].

Our sun is about 75 percent hydrogen and 25 percent helium, which is just the correct amount of energy and light to keep God's people and everything else energetic on earth[5]. That fact makes the sun the earth's best friend. This same sun that brings just the right amount of energy and light to the earth could easily fry every living thing on earth if it were just a little bit closer to us or a wee bit hotter. The average temperature on the surface of the sun is 11,000 F (6,000C[6])! One true fact is enough evidence that God created all life. Some scientists have studied the sun and say it is about five billion[7] years old, but of course, only God knows when He created all things including the sun. God made the sun in four different layers, much like our earth has layers. Just like God created the earth's valleys, mountains, and ocean beds, He also designed our sun's storms, sunspots, and solar winds.

What about You?

Without the sun, our earth and all that is on it and in it would be frozen, dead, and dark[8]. Our earth depends on our sun for warmth and growth of all living things. You can say earth is desperate for the sun because all living things need its light. Being the center of our solar system, this ball of gases is indeed our best friend.

Who in your world gives you the greatest joy? Who is your peace in a tough time? Why not ask God to give you the answers to those questions? You can thank God because He has given you all that you have. He is worthy of your trust, because the Bible says He never changes. Praise God because He sacrificed His only Son, Jesus the Christ, so you could be forgiven from your sin and receive eternal life which is grace though faith in Christ Jesus. Find today's scripture verse in your Bible and underline it.

Later Jesus talked to the people again, saying, "I am the
light of the world. The person who follows me will never live
in darkness but will have the light that gives life."
John 8:12 NCV

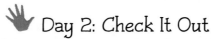 Day 2: Check It Out

The surface of the sun is about 11,000 degrees Fahrenheit (6,000

degress Celsius) and the very core or center is about 27,000,000 F (15,000,000 degrees Celsius)[9]. When we study the sun, it is full of number facts. With your parents' permission, visit the library or go online to discover five or six other mega stars. What are their names? How far away from planet earth are they? Draw and label what stars you found. What did you find out?

_____

_____

_____

☝ Day 3: Check Within

It is gravity that holds all planets together. The planets keep going around, and the gravity keeps them from flying off into space. Gravity is like the glue that God created to keep the planets revolving around their center, the sun. Read 1 John 4:13–16. Who is it that keeps you right in the middle of God's love? What did He do for you, and how does He keep doing it?

_____

_____

_____

☝ Day 4: Check Around

Many cultures throughout time have highly worshipped the sun, other planets, and animals. Because the sun brings life to the earth for living things, many have been fooled to think it was the center of life. Read Romans 1: 20–22, and 25. What have people worshipped instead of God? How do people today still worship things God created instead of Almighty God?

_____

_____

_____

 ## Day 5: Check with the Lord

Read Psalm 61:3–4, and then pray this prayer:

Lord, I am forever pulled toward You because You are the supreme force of grace. Grace is Your love for me no matter what I have done or what I have not done. You died on a cross with no sin inside You and carried all my sin to the grave. Then, three days later, You rose alive, so I would never die but live with You forever. This is the best news I've ever heard! In Jesus's name I pray, Amen.

Week 27
Where Did All the Bugs Go?

Winter's blanket of ice is on the lawn, and the trees have almost lost every leaf. The flowers seem to have crumpled up with the first frost, and now only the pansies poke their faces up from the cold and hard dirt. Maybe you have wondered where all the butterflies went that used to dance all over your backyard last summer. Overnight, they are gone, along with the grasshoppers, moths, crickets, and a bunch of other crawling critters. Where, oh where, did they go?

Migration is one way for hundreds of insects to beat the cold months. The cooler days of autumn and winter approaching signals the Monarch butterfly that it is time to leave its summer grounds and skedaddle on down to Mexico and even some to the West Indies. Some moths will also take a hint from the Monarchs and fly off to warmer climates[1]. Hibernation is another way for insects to stay alive. They will go into a larvae, pupae, or nymph stage depending on the species. The woolly bear caterpillar becomes a larvae, hiding under leaf litter to protect itself. Dragonflies or stoneflies become nymphs living down inside ponds and streams beneath the ice. They eat all winter, and when spring comes they are adults. Some moths that do not migrate like the saturniidae, will go into the pupae stage, hibernating until spring. Still other insects are created to have the water in their bodies changed into a fluid (called glycerol) that acts like antifreeze, which keeps water from freezing solid in car radiators. [2]

No matter the species of insect, they need to find habitats to hide inside because most insect bodies cannot work or eat in extreme cold. During a wintery day, carefully look inside logs or tree holes and even under rocks where the soil has stayed dry. If you find an insect, be careful to not touch or disturb it. Re-covering it as you found the little critter will assure its protection.

What about You?

God has a plan for every sort of insect. He should. He designed each one. Either they go away to warmer weather or shut down their bodies to keep quiet until spring.

On the days that do not go your way, and the door shuts down on your plans, do you pout and get mad? Maybe you stop, think, and ask the Lord Jesus what He wants you to do or where He wants you to go. If you have not prayed, ask your Counselor, the Lord Jesus Christ, how you can be willing to do what He wants you to do and not just what you want to do. This is trust and an attitude of trust pleases God and makes your life less stressed. Find today's scripture verses in your Bible and underline them.

Trust in the Lord with all your heart; do not depend
on your own understanding. Seek his will in all you
do, and he will show you which path to take.
Proverbs 3:5–6 NLT

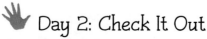 Day 2: Check It Out

Under the blanket of snow the temperature is amazingly steady. This steady or average temperature keeps the bugs alive until the air temperature rises[3]. With your parents' permission, visit the library or go online to find which insects live in your state. Choose three which hibernate under the snow and rocks. Then choose two that migrate. What did you find out?

_____

_____

_____

🖐 Day 3: Check Within

God often works through what might seem insignificant or small things to bring you closer to Himself. Why? Read Exodus 2:1–10 and 3:11–12. God saved baby Moses so He might do big things through him. What did God tell Moses when Moses said he was nobody? What small things do you see the Lord doing in your life recently that can bring you closer to Him?

_____

_____

_____

🖐 Day 4: Check Around

This winter when you look under rocks and under icy fence rails, you may find a miracle of God—a dead-looking bug, yet it is asleep, waiting to wake up and begin again. Read Matthew 9:35–38. Jesus knows how much you want your friend to become a Christian. How can you be prepared for Jesus to use you today as an example of Himself to help another kid find a new start in Him? Can you stop and help that kid that might be unorganized or how about the new kid who is looking for a friend?

_____

_____

_____

 ## Day 5: Check with the Lord

Pray this prayer:

Dear Lord, I see how gentle You are when I see the tiny birds tucked inside a bush during the rainstorm. When I hear of earthquakes and floods, I know You are the One who controls all things and makes all things work together for the good of those who love You. I do not understand a lot of things in my life, but I am at rest knowing You are guiding my every footstep. There is no better place than that, Jesus. I want that for my friends. I want them to know You. In Jesus's name I pray, Amen.

Write your own short prayer asking God to make a way so you can lovingly share with that special friend how Jesus has become your Savior and Lord.

Week 28
Snow Geese: V=Victory

During the fall and spring, you might check out the big blue skies for some pretty amazing moving "V" shapes! Snow geese breed in the Arctic tundra, and then, because of loss of food and the cold, they spend winters on farmlands in America's south, southwest, and east coasts. During the change of the seasons, migration is on the snow goose's list of things to do. Their round trips are about 5,000 miles (8,046.72 km).[1]

It is hard not to hear a gaggle of geese as they wing their way in a V formation toward more comfortable weather. Scientists have found many reasons for this V formation. Much has to do with teamwork. From this formation the geese can communicate well with one another. As they wing their way onward each goose will honk support now and then to the lead goose. The lead goose listens to its buddies' encouraging honks. With each wing flap, the air behind that wing immediately helps the bird just behind it and so on across the formation. That uplift or updraft allows the geese to migrate 71 percent further than if each bird flew alone! [2]

At traveling speeds of over 50 mph (80.47 kph) [3] the lead goose works very hard continuously because it does not have the updraft of another bird. The encouraging honks from each bird are what keep the lead goose doing its strenuous job one flap after another. When the lead gooses tires, it just pops out of the lead and rotates back into formation, and another goose takes its place in the lead position, which gets hit the hardest by the oncoming winds. If a goose should get sick or injured and fall out of the V, two of the team will follow it down out of the sky to provide protection as they all three hopefully land in a safe place[4].

The V formation allows the birds to glide more often, which saves the energy (up to 50 percent) of each bird allowing for more rests along their migration[5]. Just like fighter pilots in the same formation, they can keep track of one another much easier than if in a straight line.

What about You?

Bird observers have found that, after migration, the birds do not break up but form strong family units until they return again to their breeding grounds[6]. Like geese helping one another, you can listen to your friends with care. How can you listen to your friends? How about by keeping eye contact when you talk together, being patient when they talk, or keeping headphones out of your ears? To be a friend, you need to treat others like you want to be treated. Geese are a team and you and your friends are a team, helping when one of you falls "out of formation."

The Bible says friends are gifts from God. A gaggle (or bunch) of friends is not always what is important, but the kind of friend you are, *is* important. Are you an encouraging friend? Ask God to help you to eagerly help your friends even when it might be hard or an inconvenience. Find today's scripture verses in your Bible and underline them.

Two people are better than one, for they can help each other succeed. If one person falls, the other can reach out and help. But someone who falls alone is in real trouble.
Ecclesiastes 4:9–10 NLT

🖐 Day 2: Check It Out

With your parents' permission, visit the library or go online to find out more about snow geese migration. Five thousand miles is a long way. Look on a map and find which "fly way" they travel. What is a "fly way"? The V formation definitely brings these mighty birds success. What did you find out?

_____

_____

_____

🖐 Day 3: Check Within

The goose that drops out of the V formation will feel a huge drag or powerful resistance. Why? Read Philippians 2:1–5. God knows you need others as much as they need you. If you have God inside of you He directs your "fly way." Were you careful to ask God into your plans today? What might you need from your friend or family today? Who can you ask for help or encouragement today?

_____

_____

_____

🖐 Day 4: Check Around

Philippians 2:4 is like a picture of the gaggle of snow geese. Looking out for one another will bring success in the journey. Do not look out for your own self but be interested in others. How did Paul explain that in Philippians 2:4? What might you stop asking for from your parents or what might you stop doing that is upsetting to them, so you can do as Jesus would today?

_____

_____

_____

Day 5: Check with the Lord

Read Psalm 37:4, and then pray this prayer:

Lord, sometimes I struggle with being a team player. I know what I need to do, but I do not do it. Thank You for dying on that cross and taking my sin away. The Bible says You have removed my sin as far as the east is from the west. That makes me glad! I want to love those who You love. Sometimes I get jealous of the attention my friend gets. I don't like feeling that way. The more I read my devotional and my Bible, the more I learn to be the child of God You want me to be. In Jesus's name I pray, Amen.

Week 29
Northern California Living Giants

There is a living giant that has been standing for at least 1,200 years[1]. Along with its fellow giants, this mighty creation of God is an awesome sight when you stand beside it and look way up. What or who is this giant?

Coastal Redwood trees cluster in colossal groves off the foggy coasts of northern California, USA. In the Redwood National Parks on the California coast lives the tallest measured tree to date (2011). Hyperion was titled the tallest tree alive in August of 2006. This living giant stands 371.9 feet (113 meters). The Statue of Liberty is 305 (92.96 meters) feet from the base to the top of Lady Liberty's torch. The Sequoia sempervirens species live between 1,200–1,800 years or more[2]. What year did Columbus discover the Americas? This tree was already growing for many years when Columbus came to America.

How can these trees grow so tall and live for centuries? God has made these living giants with unique tools or survival parts. One of the giant Redwoods' tools is their root systems. The roots are sent *out* and not *down* into the ground. The roots will shoot out away from the tree, and be as long as three times the height of the tree. A 300-foot-tall (91.44 meters) redwood's roots will go out underground some 900 feet (274.32 meters). If you could see underground, you would see roots and more roots all mixed up so that all the underground is almost all wooden[3]. Coastal Redwoods find their true strength, endurance, and health, not in themselves, but because each tree lives with hundreds of others called clusters.

What about You?

Coastal Redwoods need many things to be the survivors that they are. God has made them to live in clusters of gigantic support. Standing alone is not good for a California coastal Redwood.

Your family is your support. Sometimes you might believe that you can take care of all the things in your life without anyone's help. Like the giant trees, God did not create you to live without others. God made you to be stronger when you are with others that love God. The kids in your church or Sunday school are also a God-given strength, like family. You might not know it now, but you too are strength for someone that you may not even know. When times get rough, the church is like the Redwood roots woven tightly together as your buddies encourage you and you encourage them to stand strong on Jesus's promises. Find today's scripture verses in your Bible and underline them.

*Two people are better than one… If one falls down, the
other can help him up. But it is bad for the person who
is alone and falls, because no one is there to help.
Ecclesiastes 4: 9a-10 NCV*

Day 2: Check It Out

Hyperion holds the record of the tallest recorded living tree to date (2011). With your parent's permission, visit the library or go online to find out what kind of weather helps these giants stay alive and grow so tall. What do Helios, Icarus, and Stratosphere Giants have in common? What did you find out?

_____

_____

_____

🖐 Day 3: Check Within

Back in the early 1900s, these trees were named sempervirens which means in Latin, "everlasting" or "evergreen." Everything alive will die one day, even the mighty Coastal Redwood trees. Read Isaiah 40:28–31. Who has been and will be forever? Who or what does scripture say you need to renew your strength?

_____

_____

_____

🖐 Day 4: Check Around

When a Redwood falls, its bark is slowly transformed into habitats for critters of all sizes. Read Romans 8:28. Just like all parts of the tree are used by little animals after it has fallen, so too, are all your good times and tough times made to work for your good and for God's glory. Which friend or family member might need to hear this truth today?

_____

_____

_____

 # Day 5: Check with the Lord

Pray this prayer:

Dear Lord, thank You for all parts of my life. The happy and good things seem so easy to thank You for. I want to learn to thank You always and for how You will change and grow me through tough problems or disappointments. Like those roots that go out and mix with each other for strength, please help me to place my faith and trust only in You! The Bible lets me know that You work always for my good and your glory. Lord, when bad things happen next time, I will remember that You are working for me no matter what. You are making me just like You. In Jesus' name I pray, Amen.

Write your own short prayer thanking God that He died for you and all your sin, and then ask Him to help with whatever it is you need of Him.

132

Week 30
High-Tech Ears

Sounds… we hear them wherever we go. Or do we? We hear a sound because something or someone makes a sound. But wait, is that the way it goes? Next time you are at the zoo, check out the elephants. These big guys look chilled out and silent. In fact you might get bored watching these quiet giants. But you will be surprised to know they have a secret!

God has given elephants (and many other animals) ears that hear sounds which we cannot. Infrasound is a low-pitched sound on the range or spectrum of sounds which some animals can hear and use to their benefit. The elephants' high-tech ears can hear this sound. The next time you visit the zoo you might be able to see an elephant "doing" infrasound. The place between its eyes will flutter or throb. Infrasound is a low, weird throbbing in the air around you, more like a feeling than a sound; you might call them vibes. This mysterious sound or vibration travels through the elephants' sinus cavity.

Elephants will choose to use infrasound when they are trying to tell one another something. In the wild, these huge mammals hang out in groups in the forests of Asia and the grasslands of Africa. Because the bulls (males) and cows (females) live separately and, many times, far away from one another, they use this infrasound to find one another so they can mate. They also use this quiet sound to pass life-saving messages from group to group. If a watering hole has dried up, a group of elephants will send a message such as, "Don't waste your energy coming here!" Or sometimes lightning will cause their food supply to be scorched and gone, so the same message will be sent letting their families know to go to another food source[1]. The infrasound waves travel through the ground or low to the ground for several miles[2].

Like email, phone, or text, the elephants can stay connected. If the wind is blowing in the wrong direction, they will not be able to pick up the scent, so they just turn up their high-tech ears to listen for infrasound. The Lord's creation is so full of exciting works, but we have to look for them to appreciate each.

What about You?

Most of the time infrasound travels through the ground and, without fading away, takes the elephants' messages many miles until they reach the ears of their families. The sound is strong and understandable, though it is silent.

Did you know you can talk aloud or silently to Jesus anytime, anyplace, and He will hear? But just like the elephant's secret language, you have to have the ears of your heart ready to hear the Lord. When you invite Jesus Christ into your heart, the Holy Spirit gives you those ears to hear for the rest of your life. Then you need to listen with your heart as you read, pray, and think about what you have read in your Bible and devotional. Find today's scripture verses in your Bible and underline them.

My sheep listen to my voice; I know them, and they
follow me. I give them eternal life, and they will never
die and no one can steal them out of my hand.
John 10: 27–28 NCV

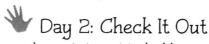 Day 2: Check It Out

Asking your parents' permission, visit the library or go online to find other critters that use *infra*sound. What about the animals that use *ultra*-sound giving them high-tech ears into their environments. What did you find out?

_____

_____

_____

Day 3: Check Within

To listen with high-tech ears, the elephant needs to quiet itself. What does the Bible say about listening? Read Luke 10:38–42. Jesus loved both Martha and Mary. But what did Mary do that Jesus said was the "better thing and it will never be taken from her"? What does it mean to "sit at Jesus feet and listen"?

_____

_____

_____

Day 4: Check Around

These days, kids plug iPods or cell phones into their ears almost twenty-four-seven. Keeping your ears unplugged now and then allows your ears to hear what is going on around you. Plugging yourself into some quiet time with your devotional and Bible will help you be aware of God's plans for you and your heart will hear God speak to it. How can you get your buddies to unplug once and a while so they can listen to what God wants to tell them?

_____

_____

_____

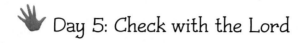 Day 5: Check with the Lord

Read Psalm 27:14, and then pray this prayer:

Dear Lord, thank You for giving me a new start to my day, my attitude, my choices, and my desire to please You. Just knowing that You want me to sit and be with You make these few minutes with You worthwhile! Lord, help me with all I need to do today. I need You to keep watch over my thinking and my words! Teach me how to turn off the wrong things in my daily life, like Martha needed to learn. I want to listen for You as You speak to my heart. Teach me to have high-tech ears inside my heart to listen for Your voice. In Jesus's name I pray, Amen.

Week 31
Death Valley=Mega Hot!

There is one place in the Western Hemisphere that is almost 300 feet (91.44 m) below sea level, and yet you could stand there and not be under water. Death Valley, California is called a desert or an arid region. The summers in this place are some of the hottest recorded on earth. One summer, in 1913, the temperature reached 134°F. (56.67°C).[1] Death Valley, California got its grim name for obvious reasons.

Death Valley has mega-hot temperatures that have caused animals and plants living in the 3,000-square-mile (7,770 sq. km) desert to adapt or change over many years. The extreme heat brings tests of endurance to the animals' bodies and their habitats. Everyone needs to drink water, even rats and snakes, right? Not so. Kangaroo rats munch on dry seeds in the desert, and that is enough. Along with kidneys that work overtime to conserve water, their bodies remove water from the fat and starch inside the seeds they eat. Death Valley is not going to do the kangaroo rat in! He can go his whole life without drinking a drop of water. Like many of the desert critters, this little guy sleeps inside the ground in burrows by day, keeping out of the scorching sun's heat. Nighttime is the right time to search for food, keeping his body from overheating and saving him energy. Before settling in for his sleep at the end of the evening's hunt, he may even block the passage of his house with dirt, keeping it cooler and free of any lurking enemy[2].

The sidewinder rattlesnake is another survivor. It forms loops with its legless body, throwing itself forward quickly as it gets from place to place on the hot desert floor. Reptiles like the sidewinder live best in the hot and arid desert. Like the kangaroo rat, these rattlesnakes do not need a drink of water their entire life. The snake hopes the kangaroo rat will leave his burrow open, so the snake might find a juicy lunch. The snake's body draws the liquid from the rat's body and delivers it to the snake's important body organs[3]. God has made adaptations for the little critters living in the deathly hot valley of extremes to survive. Because of their adaptations, the insects, birds, reptiles, and mammals living in Death Valley have become stronger than the same species in climates that are not so hot.

What about You?

When the heat gets too hot in Death Valley, the critters shut down and hide from the blazing sun. Family, friends, and school can bring tough problems and concerns. Like the Death Valley animals, you might feel tempted to retreat or shut down but not by running or hiding or ignoring your frustrations. Retreat into your faith that whispers to your thoughts: "God is working inside my problem. He is listening to my real concerns, so I can trust Him moment by moment."

In fact, problems make you a stronger person, because it is in problems that you want to call out to God. He wants you to call to Him so you can know Him as your Rock of protection and strength. He is also your hiding place where you can share everything inside your heart. Just as the kangaroo rat and sidewinder have found relief from the burning sun, you can find relief from your problems by placing your faith and trust in the One who knows your name. Find today's scripture verses in your Bible and underline them.

Give Me Five for Fangs, Feathers, and Faith!

Rescue me from my enemies, Lord; I run to you to hide me.
Psalm 143:9 NLT

From the ends of the earth, I cry to you for help when my heart
is overwhelmed. Lead me to the towering rock of safety.
Psalm 61:2 NLT

🖐 Day 2: Check It Out

Sidewinder rattlesnakes are poisonous. Unlike boas and other constrictor snakes, the sidewinder uses its poisonous venom to kill its prey. With your parents' permission, visit the library or go online to discover your state's poisonous snakes. How many did you find? Where in your state are most of these poisonous snakes located? If you can visit your local zoo, be sure to check out snake house!

🖐 Day 3: Check Within

Though Death Valley blazes with heat, there is God's protection and provision or care, inside of the valley. The kangaroo rat has no water to drink, yet God gives it more than enough water from the food it eats. Read about Elijah, the prophet in 1 Kings 17:8–16. God provides for you, like the widow in the story, in ways you do not expect. In what ways has the Lord helped you when you had thought it was impossible to change your circumstance?

Day 4: Check Around

Please re-read 1 Kings 17:8–16 passage. The widow in Zarephath and her son were about to give up and die. What did Elijah ask her to do that required her to have much faith in God? What was the important life-saving lesson she learned? What friend of yours has felt like nothing is working, and it all seems hopeless? Ask God to give you the right moment to share this story with your friend!

_____

_____

_____

Day 5: Check with the Lord

Pray this prayer:

Lord, thank You for giving me my faith, so I can see Your love even when I don't see anything good going on. When I obey in faith, this story tells me You will supply Your perfect solution for me. Even though I can't see the solution, please reassure my heart, Lord, so I can believe You are in each problem or fear that comes in my life. God, please give me a way to share Your love with my friend. In Jesus' name I pray, Amen.

Write your own short prayer thanking God that He can quiet your heart from your worries. Ask Him to do just that the next time you get afraid.

Week 32
The Camel-God's Desert Taxi

If your family needed to move to Africa's Sahara Desert, the first thing to pick up at the local desert shop might be a camel. Why? Maybe because the desert is hot, has unsteady sand dunes that go on and on, and water is not exactly at your finger tips. Dromedary camels are like having access to a taxi anytime you want it on a blazing hot summer's day.

This one-humped dromedary camel will take you where you want to go. The unstable sand dunes of the desert are no match for the camel's wide-split hooves[1]. This strong mammal can carry about 990 pounds (450kg) but a usual and more comfortable load is 330 pounds (150kg). When the wind begins to blow, it creates blinding and painful sand storms. But a camel's long and thick eyelashes, ear hairs, and nose hairs help to filter out the desert stinging sands. God even created its nose to close up in times of severe sand storms. He also designed a slit that runs from its nose to its mouth which collects any mucous that might be lost! Yuck!

Got a thirst? Camel's milk can be used fresh or left to turn to a curd state like cottage cheese. Our body needs vitamin C for many reasons. Vegetables and fruits have lots of vitamin C, but the desert sands make it hard for these plants to grow. Camel's milk is the answer for people living in the desert. The camel comes to the rescue, because its milk is loaded (unlike cows' milk) with vitamin C[2].

Long periods without water are no problem for this fearless mammal. Even with heavy packs on its back, a camel can manage for seventeen days or so without any water or food[3]. How? This huge and hard-working mammal hardly sweats. Sweating is how many mammals die because of loss of water from their bodies. Hurray for the bumps and the humps. The hump on his back stores fat deposits. When food or water gets scarce, the fat will mix with oxygen in its blood, breaking the fat into water to be used throughout the camel's body[4]. The challenges of the burning-hot sands of the desert are no match for this tough survivor.

What about You?

The dromedary camel is custom-created for the hot places on earth. The Bible does not say for sure that the wise men had camels when they visited the Christ child, but being wise, they probably did.

You need to be wise when it comes to using the body God gave you. Thank Him for the mind He gave you. No matter if you are disabled and unable to do what you want or not, your mind enables you to make choices for the body God gave you. He gave you your stomach, legs, hands, seven body systems, and a heart. How best can you praise God with what He has given you? One way is to put good things into your mind and body while keeping unhealthy thinking, junk food, and drugs out of your body. When Jesus Christ comes to live in you, He will slowly show you ways to care for yourself. Thank Him now for this blessing. Find today's scripture verses in your Bible and underline them.

You should know that your body is a temple for the Holy Spirit who is in you. You have received the Holy Spirit from God. So you do not belong to yourselves. (20) because you were bought by God for a price. So honor God with your bodies.
1 Corinthians 6:19–20 NCV

Day 2: Check It Out

God has given the camel amazing adaptations in order to survive in its desert habitats around the world. With your parents' permission, visit the library or go online to find out how many years camels have been helping people in deserts and how many species of camel there are. What did you find out?

_____

_____

_____

Day 3: Check Within

The camel lives in a tough world; deserts can be dangerous. But God has given it body *armor,* keeping it strong, highly respected by desert folks, courageous, and victorious over its environment. Read Ephesians 6:13–18. Where does your courage and hope come from? What does Paul mean in verse 18 when we says, "always keep on praying?"

_____

_____

_____

Day 4: Check Around

There is no doubt about it; camels can carry loads of weight in extreme conditions and not worry about it. Wherever people go, their loads of things go with them and their worries too. We carry loads with us sometimes too—our worries. Read Matthew 11: 28–30. Do you have a special friend who you worry about? What does Jesus say He wants you to do with your concerns?

_____

_____

_____

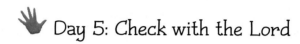 ## Day 5: Check with the Lord

Read Psalm 27: 5–6, and then pray this prayer:

Lord Jesus, You are my burden-bearer. There is no load of problems or fears that You cannot carry for me! The camel reminds me that I do not have to be afraid. So many times I keep thinking and worrying about everything that hurts my heart. Your Word tells me that I can come to You with my worries and concerns and leave them with You. So I choose to do that today, God, because You care about every single thing I care about. Thank You Jesus for being right here always to hear me. In Jesus's name I pray, Amen.

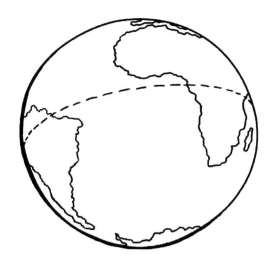

Week 33
Forecast: Humid and Hot

Summer is an awesome time of year! We can put sweaters and jackets back in the closets and get out last years shorts (if they fit), t-shirts, and swimwear! In winter we need more clothing for obvious reasons. Weather can really affect our activities and our day's plans, unless of course you live where the weather is the same twenty-four-seven.

"Hot, humid, and a chance for rain" is what you would hear the weatherman say every day if you lived in rainforests on the equator. The equator passes through thirteen countries: Ecuador, Colombia, Brazil, Sao Tome & Principe, Gabon, Congo, the Democratic Republic of the Congo, Uganda, Kenya, Somalia, Maldives, Indonesia, and Kiribati[1]. Even though the rainforests give way to high mountains that do get snow on their tops, the rest of the rainforests are hot and humid and rainy all the time. The rainforests have 80–430 inches (203.2 cm–1,092.2 cm) of rain per year depending on the forest's location, the winds, the land, and thickness of trees in the forest[2]. This 25,000-mile (40,233.33 km) circumference of the earth (the equator) is where more than half the earth's plants and animals live and hang out. These forests cover only 6 percent of the surface of our earth.

All these equator countries have only two seasons and no daylight savings time. The people have no need to think about what to wear that day. That is because places near the equator receive twelve hours of solar or sun energy, 365 days a year. The rest of the earth has seasons. As the earth tilts in its rotation around the sun during one year, the sunlight will be longer and stronger on one side of the equator. This tilting creates the spring and then summer seasons[3]. Then the earth will slowly tilt away from the sun, and that area will have less sunlight and solar energy[4]. That is wintertime. But no matter how the earth tilts, the equator or middle line of the earth always collects the same amount of sunlight.

What about You?

Now, the earth has done this back-and-forth rotation thing twenty-four hours a day, seven days a week, and 365 days a year for millions of years. It's always been the same since God said, "Let there be light." All those equator countries are full of busy people with jobs, families, and even problems that bother them. One thing they know will not take them by surprise is the humid, hot, rainy weather.

The God of the universe, the one and only God who is always the same yesterday, today, and forever, created the earth and all things in it. Praise and thank the Lord now for keeping our planet in His perfect care. But also thank Him because His protection goes before you and keeps you from things that you have no idea may be wrong for you! His knowledge and wisdom not only keep the whole universe in place but keep your deepest concerns in His own heart! Find today's scripture verse in your Bible and underline it.

Let everything that has breath praise the Lord. Praise the Lord.
Psalm 150:6

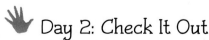 Day 2: Check It Out

The rainforests along the equator are home to over half of the earth's plants and animals. There are many animals living around the equator that have yet to be discovered. With your parents' permission, visit the library or go online to find one or two animals or plants that live solely in equator countries. What did you find?

_____

_____

_____

🖐 Day 3: Check Within

Even though the equatorial rainforests have constant heat and light in the daytime, most of the forest floor or bottom is very dark. But climb up to the top of one of the trees (maybe 200 feet or 60.96 meters) and what might be up there? Read John 3:19–21. Why did people love darkness in Jesus's time and even now? What do you think Jesus meant by light and dark in this passage?

_____

_____

_____

🖐 Day 4: Check Around

People can change their minds. But God never changes. Read James 1:17. What does this verse say that God is like? You can believe that God will always guide and love you exactly the same no matter what. Which of your family members might need to hear from you today about James 1:17? What words might you use to share this truth?

_____

_____

_____

Day 5: Check with the Lord

Pray this prayer:

Dear Lord, the Bible says You are always the same. Everyday my emotions are changing and sometimes they get me into trouble! You promise to be with me always even when I don't feel You are there. If I were deep in the darkest forest, You would be there with me. When I feel left out or my friends don't understand me, You are constantly with me and on my side! Thank You Lord Jesus, that You are the Light of the World. In Jesus's name I pray, Amen.

Write your own short prayer first thanking God that He hears you and then asking Him for whatever you have been praying about.

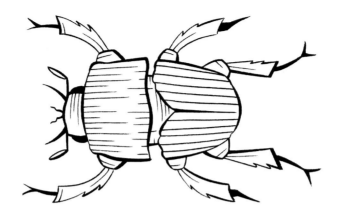

Week 34
Nature's Clean-Up Crew

Going for a walk on a summer night can be an adventure. Make sure the front door is shut tightly as you leave. Why? The moths, salamanders, and June bugs are crawling and flying around your warm porch light. Watch out or they will zip past that open door and into your house lamps.

The June bug has a cousin, the dung beetle, who would think hanging around porch lights is boring. The June and dung beetles are a part of a humongous family of beetles called scarab beetles. This big family makes up 10 percent (30,000) of all the beetles that have so far been discovered in the world. Herbivores are animals that eat plants. Their undigested food is called dung. Dung is what interests this little black bug. The dung beetles have a big-time job. They are preoccupied with dung and always will be. Down in Texas, the farmers love these little guys. The useful dung beetle will bury some 80 percent of the cattle dung[1].

This little black critter lives on all continents except Antarctica, and the desert, and the tundra[2]. With their highly-tuned sense of smell, they will find dung, and with their custom mouth parts, they will zap up the liquid and nutrients left in the undigested herbivore dung. Some dung beetles will just live in the dung. Working in pairs, they begin with a small piece of dung and roll it over and over with their back legs until it is many times larger than themselves. Soon, the ball of dung is buried, and they begin again. Mom dung beetles will lay one egg inside a dung ball. She leaves her egg alone as it grows into a mature beetle, all the while munching on the dung as it grows. Then, when the food supply is about eaten up, the critter will just walk off[3]. Can you guess what is on the menu at the next meal?

What about You?

This dung-ball making beetle is a big-time hero as it moves so much waste underground, controlling disease and pests among livestock all over the world. Different types of dung beetles have different jobs, and so do you. What sort of job might you do? God gives you talents and spiritual gifts which work together to work for God's plans and your plans. Even though you are young, God will begin to show you what these gifts and talents are when you have fellowship with other Christian kids and adults. You will experience what real love, joy, peace, patience, kindness, goodness, faithfulness, gentleness, and self-control are. These fruits of the Spirit bless your friends and family as you learn to use them. Find today's scripture verse in your Bible and underline it.

As each part does its own special work, it helps the other parts grow,
so that the whole body is healthy and growing and full of love.
Ephesians 4:16 NLT

Day 2: Check It Out

The dung beetle is hard-working recycler. How is that? As they bury the dung balls, the soil is turned over and over again. With your parents' permission, visit the library or go online to find out how the dung beetle is a farmer's great friend. Hint: it is all about bugs! What did you find out?

_____

_____

_____

🖐 Day 3: Check Within

Dweller dung beetles are content to stay on top of the dung, lay eggs, and raise their young. Read 2 Chronicles 29: 1–6. Hezekiah did not just sit on top of the "dung" or the corruption. What did he do? Where in your thinking and heart do you need to clean up the way you think, talk, or act? What names do you call your sister or brother that you can stop doing? What bad words or negative thinking about schoolwork might you stop doing?

_____

_____

_____

🖐 Day 4: Check Around

Read 2 Chronicles 31:1, 20–21. The Israelites did as Hezekiah told them. They destroyed all that was destroying their relationship with the holy God. Hezekiah came against anything that was against God. You too can become a supporter for God's work. Instead of finding fault with a kid or joining in to make fun of others, how can you be like Hezekiah?

_____

_____

_____

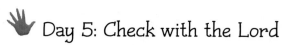

Day 5: Check with the Lord

Read Psalm 111:10, and then pray this prayer:

Dear Lord, thank You for bringing me the story of Hezekiah. No matter how weird or funny things look to me, I know You are right in the middle of it. Even dung beetles can teach me how to live for You and be a better friend to my friends. Please keep working in my heart, transforming it so I can be a forgiving person. Remind me each day to first pray and then with Your power, stand against mean and bad things. In Jesus's name I pray, Amen.

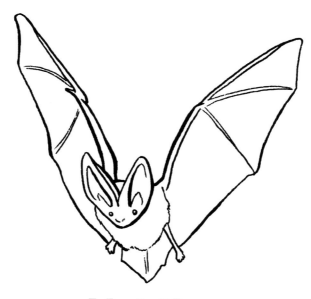

Week 35
Bats Get a Bad Rap!

For thousands of years, bats have been stuck with not-so-nice names. They've been called friends of witches, evil vampires, ghost buddies, and blood suckers. Even ideas like bats get tangled in your hair, bats are dirty, or they always carry rabies have kept the truth about bats from most people down through the centuries[1]. But God intended this little critter for a nighttime sort of life, which probably did not help its reputation.

But good news—the bat has a lot to offer the earth. The bat is one of God's top-notch creations. Why? Bats hear high-pitched noises and communicate like submarines. Ultrasound is their guidance system. Called echolocation, the insect-eating bats make high-pitched squeaks allowing for sound waves to bounce off anything as it wings its way through the night sky. Insect swarms, trees, and flowers are detected by the bat's high-tech ears[2]. Even objects as thin as a human hair are easily navigated in the dark of night. The old saying, "blind as a bat" is another false title because flying fruit bats (flying foxes) use their sight more than their ears to locate fruits and flowers hundreds of times a night[3].

Among the 1,200 species of bats, all but three eat insects, small animals like frogs and rodents, fruit, or nectar. The other three species are vampire bats, which are found in South America[4]. In just one night, a single insect-eating bat can gobble three thousand insects, helping farmers keep their cattle and sheep free of disease. Instead of costly, dangerous insecticides, many farmers breed bats to eat up disease-carrying insects that would have bitten their livestock. The fruit bats also fertilize thousands of plants each night as they wing their way from flower to flower. As flying foxes sip pollen, they unknowingly swoosh their little faces in the pollen thus fertilizing hundreds of species of flowers each night[5].

What about You?

Bats got nasty names from the false information spread about them. Has anyone ever called you a not-so-nice name? Do you know someone who tells stories about kids just to poke fun? That is called gossiping.

Jesus told people not to gossip. Our Savior was belittled and gossiped about even though he did no wrong, ever. When you have been hurt by others calling you a name, God wants to give you the same comfort He gave Jesus. Always remember that if you have anything to say about anyone, let it be good. When you give your heart to Jesus Christ, the Holy Spirit will give you kind and loving words to encourage others instead of nasty name-calling or gossiping. Find today's scripture verse in your Bible and underline it.

My children, we should love people not only with words
and talk, but by our actions and true caring.
1 John 3: 18 NCV

Day 2: Check It Out

Bats come out at night. The darkness brings out all sorts of animals that are not seen in the day. With your parents' permission, visit the library or go online to find out about some Australian mammals like the Tasmanian devil and the echidna. What did you find out that you did not already know?

_____

_____

_____

✋ Day 3: Check Within

Bats have been tagged with a not-so-nice reputation. Speaking the truth in love is what God calls us to do. Read Proverbs 10:19–21. What does the scripture say about your tongue? How is it able to help you keep a good reputation?

_____

_____

_____

✋ Day 4: Check Around

God created amazing ways of keeping our earth in order and working together. You too can help keep your friends by working together to stay friends. Read Proverbs 15:1–2. Like fertilizing bats do a great service to flowers, your words and actions rub off on other kids. Do your words bring order (calmness) or fighting? What can you do or say when fighting happens with your friends?

_____

_____

_____

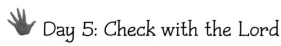 Day 5: Check with the Lord

Pray this prayer:

O Lord God, let me hear from You today! You speak to my heart when I read Your Word. Thank You for your Spirit that continues to teach me to listen for You inside my heart. I love You so much! You are always showing me the same lessons over and over because You know I am forever forgetful and slow to remember! In Jesus's name I pray, Amen.

Write your own short prayer asking God to never stop teaching you to be kind with your words and honest with your actions.

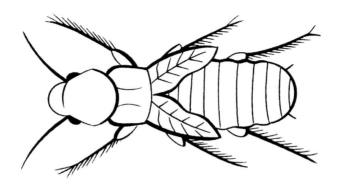

Week 36
Two Are Better Than One

There are more species of insects in the world at any one time than any other animal group. Just take a look outside. They are in all habitats of the world[1]. Although most insects live alone, the termites are one of the few species of insects that work as a team[2]. Thousands of different species or kinds of termites are busy working, breeding, and making colonies all over the world. Termites live in moist and dark places. These tiny wonders live and act like ants. There are queens and kings, repairers, foragers, workers, and soldiers living together underground in a well-ordered colony. After the queen and king mate, they begin laying millions of eggs yearly. Most species of soldier and worker (repairer) termites living in Africa or Australia work throughout their lives, building up giant palaces filled with their millions of family members[3].

African termite homes or mounds are often 10–15 feet (3–4.5 meters) in height (a record is 42 feet high (13 meters)) and made of termite spit, soil, waste, and fungus. As long as the queen and king are alive and stay inside the mound, the colony will keep growing, and the workers will add to this mound and repair any damages year after year. The queen can live up to twenty years, continually laying millions of eggs before she dies. Mounds can stay busy for up to one hundred years with new queens and kings moving in and continuing the work! Mounds see a lot of families come and go[4].

Termites will leave their mounds only when the queen stops laying eggs or dies. Once the termites die off, then the mound is open for any animals to set up housekeeping. Warthogs, porcupines, dwarf Mongooses, Black Mambas, and Spotted Hyenas are just a few burrowing animals making use of someone's left-over home. Plant seeds also find the soil moist and fertile, so they can begin to grow and stay safe because the mound is raised up off the ground. Just like people move and their homes get a new house owner, so termites give up their homes to larger critters[5]. Aren't you glad you are a person instead of a termite!

What about You?

Termite mounds take a lot of workers. Without the mound of termite team buddies, African termites would be eaten, and their eggs would be blown away in the wind. Termite mounds protect these tiny insects as they work hard to build their gigantic society.

When you do God's work, you might not have millions of workers alongside you, but the Bible says the Holy Spirit is inside you if you have asked Jesus into your heart. The Holy Spirit gives you joy, especially when you do God's work. Sometimes, the work can be hard, but just like the termite's hard work is rewarding (with a huge palace of dirt), God's work will reward you beyond all you can imagine. Have you ever worked and sung to Jesus at the same time? Praise and thank the Lord Jesus because He gives you the ability to work and enjoy it at the same time. All you have and receive comes from God. Find today's scripture verse in your Bible and underline it.

Praise the Lord O my soul. I will praise the Lord all my
life; I will sing praise to my God as long as I live.
Psalm 146:1

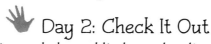

Day 2: Check It Out

Termites are tiny and almost blind, yet they live busy lives making and repairing some of the tallest and weirdest-shaped homes in Africa. With your parents' permission, visit the library or go online to find two different critters of your choice that move into empty termite mounds. Check out YouTube for African termite mound videos. What did you find out?

_____

_____

_____

Day 3: Check Within

In Africa, termites build up mighty fortresses, but when they come into human homes, they begin to destroy that home, bringing destruction and turmoil. Read Proverbs 10:20, 13:3, and 21:23. The tongue has the power to build up a friend or ruin that same friend. What sort of advice have you given lately? Did it help or hurt the kid? How can you keep from hurting someone when you're mad?

_____

_____

_____

Day 4: Check Around

Termites' power lies in their numbers. Read Hebrews 4:12. The Word of God is all power. Think about it. The words of the Bible keep working and never stop. That is why it is living. The Bible's words can change

159

hearts, and minds, and all because the Word is love. Your prayers are never forgotten or ignored by the Lord. What prayers can you write to the Lord concerning your special friend?

_____

_____

_____

Day 5: Check with the Lord

Read Psalm 139:13–14, and then pray this prayer:

Lord, so many times when I get anxious, I forget that You love me so much. When I am at school or at the mall out with friends, sometimes I feel like no one even cares if I am around. It is then that I feel like one of a million termites. But I know that thought is not from You. Please remind me to have a quiet time, and when I read, remind me that You are always loving, protecting, and guiding me. What more could I need? In Jesus's name I pray, Amen.

Week 37
Big Bubba

Animals that live in extremely cold habitats instinctively know that staying warm is as important as keeping themselves off another's lunch menu. The polar bear is the exception. The icy snow storms do not blow his mind. The icy storms do not shake this fearless mammal up. He thinks nothing of and is very well adapted to the cold and icy Arctic from as extreme as 70°F below zero (-56.66°C) to 70°F (21.1 C) on a summer day. How does this land and sea predator stay warm?

A polar bear is one of God's big guys. Being one of the largest land animals, this big Bubba can be as tall as 7–9 feet (2–3 meters) standing on his back legs. He is about 800–1,500 pounds, (363.63–681.81 kg), and females are half the weight or less—300–550 pounds (136.36–250 kg). This mega bear has no natural enemies except sickness.

Fur is their first line of defense against the cold. Two sorts of fur cover their blubber. Long, oily, guard hairs that look like tiny see-through tubes are really hollow inside. Acting like a sweater, air gets trapped inside, keeping warm air next to the bear's black skin. Working as a second sweater, his black skin soaks up the sunshine, keeping Bubba still warmer. Big Bubba's second hairs are short insulating hairs. Together, both types of hair and black skin work as a team keeping big Bubba fearlessly warm[1].

Along with its fur, its blubber gives the polar bear the edge. The density or thickness of its blubber keeps the bear toasty. Blubber is fat. This blubber is unevenly distributed over its body, from 2–4 inches (5.08–10.16 cm) in thickness depending on where it is located. The polar bear even has blubber-covered feet[2]. So God has provided a total package, keeping this warm-blooded creature alive, healthy, and active all his days on earth.

What about You?

The polar bear is the king of the Arctic, and it has no natural enemies. All the bear's body parts are protected against the bone-chilling winds and icy cold. Does the bear know how blessed it is? No, animals do not have an understanding of who they are or that there is a God. But people do. We are God's only creation that has a knowledge we are alive.

God created you just as you are. He created every part of you on purpose. Do you thank the Lord for all He has given to you? He loves it when you come and talk to Him. Talk to Jesus as though He were sitting next to you! He can be your best friend. What has He given to you? He has given you parents that love you no matter what. Did God bring a special pet into your heart? How about a home? Or how about a church where you can meet your friends? Find today's scripture verses in your Bible and underline them.

I will praise you, Lord with all my heart. I will tell all the
miracles you have done. I will be happy because of you;
God Most High, I will sing praises to your name.
Psalm 9: 1–2 NCV

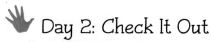 # Day 2: Check It Out

Polar bears have walked the earth since God created animals. Blubber, special hair, and God's plan have kept these beautiful animals living. With your parents' permission, visit the library or go online to find at least one of the polar bears favorite bites to eat. Why is it easy for the bear to eat it? A clue: it swims really fast. What did you discover?

_____

_____

_____

🖐 Day 3: Check Within

God creates life, and then He takes care of it or sustains it. The Lord gives just what is needed to each of His creations. God also gives believers faith so we can trust His care for us is perfect. Faith is something you can't see; faith is being sure that Jesus's promises never change. You can be sure He is GOOD all the time. Read Mark 5:21–24 and 35–43. How can you "not be afraid; just believe"?

_____

_____

_____

🖐 Day 4: Check Around

The Lord has created polar bear bodies with all they need to live well. Worry is not in the bear's plans. This big guy rests on icebergs (with eyes closed). Read Matthew 6:25–27 and 33–34. Who feeds the birds? What does Jesus say to seek or put first before all else in your life? Do you know a kid that seems scared or worries a lot? How might you encourage him?

_____

_____

_____

 ## Day 5: Check with the Lord

Pray this prayer:

Lord, when things happen that I do not understand, I choose to trust that You are in charge. I get so scared sometimes because I forget that You are already taking care of the problems for me. I want my problems to remind me that I can stop being afraid and instead believe You are working in my problem! I will wait and pray instead of obsessing on my panicked thoughts. In Jesus's name I pray, Amen.

Write your own short prayer asking God to keep
you from worry and instead praying more.

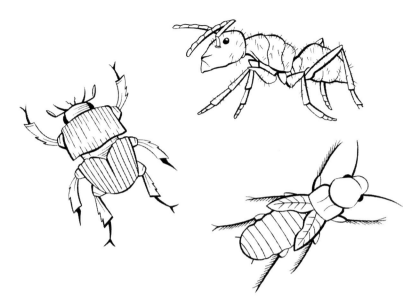

Week 38
Tiny Critters with Big Jobs

Have you gone for a walk in your neighborhood lately? Look up and down. Do you see birds? How about cats and dogs? If you live in the country, you may see deer, chipmunks, squirrels, or just about any sort of animal. Now think of all the birds that may have died around your place year after year. What about all the skunks and squirrels and tiny spiders that die yet you do not see them dead. Critters live and they die. That is God's cycle of life here on earth. What happens to all these dead critters? Why don't you see them?

God has created insects to be natural garbage disposers. At any one time, no one can know how many insects (God's scavengers) or even how many different species there are on earth. But some scientists of the Smithsonian Institute have suggested about thirty million different sorts or species and at any one moment there could be ten quintillion (10,000,000,000,000,000,000) alive on the planet earth[1]. How do you read that crazy-large number?

Insects are a part of the system God uses to decompose or break down dead things (organic matter). Insects are decomposers. They are part of a giant system of all the animals which scientists call the food chain. For example, when a sick or injured bird dies, soon an animal like a cat or opossum drops by for some lunch. Mammals, birds, reptiles, amphibians, and fish all get first dibs. The mammals usually get involved at the beginning and birds join the mammals. Then the reptiles and amphibians do their munching later. Fish would become involved if the dead bird had landed in the water. Then the remains are eaten up by ants, maggots, beetles, beetles' eggs called larvae, followed by the bacteria, which are alive but not an insect. Soon the bird is gone—totally gone. It is the same cycle with an old tree that falls in the forest. The bark soon becomes weak and the army of scavengers begins their food chain duties. Worms, grubs, army ants, paper wasps, and beetles of all sorts will soon break this massive tree down[2].

What about You?

Insects might be small, but they have monstrous jobs. Their job of eating all the things that are dead or decaying makes the world cleaner and more beautiful. To live in the world is to live in the cycle of life. No matter if you are young, middle aged, or old, God gives you a reason to be alive. Just like the insects have a job, you too can know that the Lord of heaven and earth knows you and has a special work just for you right now, today. Ask Jesus to begin to show you what it is. Be sure to write down the thoughts He begins to give to you. Find today's scripture verse in your Bible and underline it.

Guide my steps by your word, so I will not be overcome by evil.
Psalm 119:133 NLT

Day 2: Check It Out

Your neighborhood is a food chain of mammals, birds, reptiles, amphibians, insects, bacteria, and plants. With your parents' permission, go for a walk with a friend or family member and bring a notepad and pen. Look up in the sky, deep under rocks, in trees, along the bark of the tree, in bushes, in the gutters, writing down every animal you see. Later at home, place each animal in order of its place in the food chain. (Mammals, birds, reptiles, amphibians (fish), insects, bacteria/fungus). What did you discover?

_____

_____

_____

Day 3: Check Within

When living things like plants and animals die, they begin a process called decomposition. One dead tree contains more living ants, worms, beetles, mites, grubs, fungi, and bacteria than perhaps all the living trees in that one forest. Read Romans 5:12–17. Adam represents death to all God's creation. Why? What did he do? Who did Christ set free from sin when He died to sin on the cross? What have you decided to do about God's gift of grace, Jesus Christ?

_____

_____

_____

Day 4: Check Around

Many times, God uses the small and seemingly insignificant things in life to show the world the important things. Read Romans 10:8–10. God's plan of salvation is so simple that even a child can receive His grace. Jesus offers your friend, as He does you, the opportunity to trade your sin for His righteousness (goodness). Pray and ask Jesus to help you share with a friend how to receive His saving grace.

_____

_____

_____

 Day 5: Check with the Lord

Read Psalm 25:4–5, and then pray this prayer:

Lord, I think those little decomposers which clean up the world are so amazing. I see now, more than I did before, how the little things in my world are often the important things. Help me keep from thinking that I am more important than another kid. God, I know that being a friend to someone who is sad, or helping an elderly neighbor with groceries or a small job, shows them Your love. I thank and praise You, Lord, because You show me how to love others. In Jesus's name I pray, Amen.

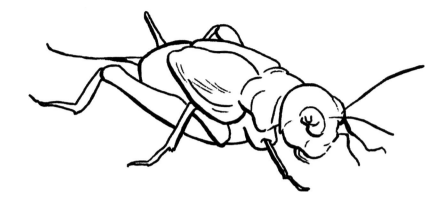

Week 39
Thermometers with Wings

Did you know crickets are cold-blooded? Cold-blooded animals like reptiles, fish, and amphibians become colder or hotter depending on the outside temperatures. Crickets have chemical reactions going on inside their bodies called activation energy. When the temperature hits 55°F (12.7°C) or above, the chemical reactions begin.

Crickets sing loud and long on hot summer nights. When the temperature is hot, a cricket's muscles are ready to rub its wings together. This action is called stridulation, which is how the male talks (chirps) to the female. The wings will rise up like a piano lid which makes that cricket song very loud. Now the top of the wing, called the scraper, is dragged across the file or underside of the other wing. This is like scraping your finger along a hair comb.

If the crickets are keeping you awake, you might as well turn on the light in your room and look at the second hand on your clock. The Farmer's Almanac is a famous book that has predicted the weather for many years. The almanac says there is a fun way to find out how warm it is on a summer's night. It recommends counting the number of chirps in fourteen seconds and then adding that number to forty. Bingo, you have discovered the tiny, cold-blooded cricket is a thermometer (in Fahrenheit) that is right- on[1].

What about You?

Just like crickets can be a gauge of temperature on a hot summer night, you too can be a gauge or indicator. How might that work? How "hot" or excited are you about Jesus? Like the crickets start chirping because it is a warm night, you too can get excited because of the Holy Spirit's power is alive inside of you.

Jesus Christ came to earth to serve others. His love is for all people. The way you act or react to situations or people shows you and them your heart attitude. Are you quick to forgive those who hurt you? Maybe you pick and choose who you want to forgive. When your mom or dad needs help, do you complain, or are you excited to go and help? Find today's scripture verse in your Bible and underline it.

Always be joyful. Never stop praying. Be thankful in all circumstances,
for this is God's will for you who belong to Christ Jesus.
1 Thessalonians 5:16–18 NLT

Day 2: Check It Out

A chemical reaction happens while combining two materials or energies that are able to react or respond together, which makes a whole new material or energy[2]. With your parents' permission, go online to: (www.sciencekids.co.nz/chemistry.html) These are fun and safe experiments for you to do. Many show you how two very different materials will make a new energy. What did you find out?

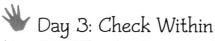 Day 3: Check Within

Read 2 Corinthians 5:17. What does it mean to be a new creation? An amazing transformation takes place, and for the rest of your life, Jesus Christ will help you and guide you. Read John 14: 16–18. How is a counselor like the Holy Spirit? Have you trusted (or believe in) Jesus Christ as your Savior? If so, how has the Holy Spirit helped you this week?

_____

_____

_____

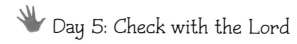 Day 4: Check Around

Read Galatians 5:22–23. This fruit is who Jesus is. He is 100 percent all of this fruit. The Lord has given you all these gifts too, but only the Holy Spirit can help you to grow or mature them inside your heart. Pray and ask the Lord how you can show your good friend the gift of patience today. How can you show your parents the gift of self-control tomorrow?

_____

_____

_____

Day 5: Check with the Lord

Pray this prayer:

O Lord God, how amazing and awesome You are! You made the whole universe. You have made little crickets with parts that have chemical reactions so they can sing. Even though You are indescribable, I can say You are the most caring God I could imagine! Though sometimes I hurt others' feelings or choose to do the wrong thing, You are there waiting to hear me confess my sin. Everyone can lose their cool with me, but You never do! Lord, you know how I want to hear You when You talk to me through the Bible. In Jesus's name I pray, Amen.

Write your own short prayer letting God know
you need His help today, once again.

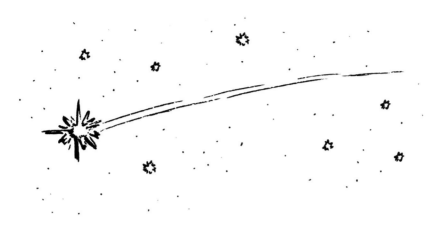

Week 40
God Is the True Light

Have you ever wondered why there is dark and why there is light? Experiments are cool. Try this experiment: close your eyes. Seems dark, right? But now, cover your eyes with both hands, keeping your eyes closed. Now, isn't that darker still? You probably could not see at all. But if you even let your eyes open a little there would be light. There would be no more darkness.

The Bible says, "In the beginning God created the heavens and the earth. Now the earth was formless and empty, darkness was over the surface of the deep, and the Spirit of God was hovering over the waters" (Genesis 1:1–2 NIV).

Stand outside on a cloudless night. Depending on whether you live in the city or the country, you will see lots of stars or only a few. The lights from the city put a haze across the starry night sky. Stars give off their own light, so they take away the dark because they shine light[1]. Why is it this way? Light is energy. You do not see the energy. You see because of the light. Take the energy away, and you have no light. You have dark.

Dark has no energy of its own[2]. Which came first? The dark or the light? If you read the Bible verse in Genesis 1:1 you would say darkness.

However, did you know that the light has *always* been? Read John 1:1–5. Do you still say darkness came first? Now re-read it again asking God to show you what it means. It says God is the Light of man. Jesus is the Word, and the Bible says as you read that He *(the Light)* was with God in the beginning. What does Genesis 1:4 say? God, being the Light, has always been first![3]

What about You?

Just like the night sky is full of millions of light-bearing stars, your life can be full of God's true Light. God's Light is Jesus Christ come to us on earth as God. The Bible says, "Later, Jesus talked to the people again, saying, I am the light of the world… " (John 8:12, NCV)

No matter how difficult things seem or how many problems you have, you can have Jesus who is the Light. His Spirit is like a gentle whisper inside overpowering your own thoughts, reminding you just how to handle things that come your way each day. But like those stars shining from within themselves, you need Jesus to shine from *within* you. When you ask Jesus to come into your heart, He will instantly fill you with His Holy Spirit. Then you will begin to know His love, wisdom, strength, and power through a relationship with Him. Find today's scripture verse in your Bible and underline it.

Here is the message we have heard from Christ and now announce
to you: God is light, and in Him there is no darkness at all.
1 John 1:5 NCV

Day 2: Check It Out

Looking up and deep into the dark, you cannot help but wonder about all those stars. How do stars make their own light? The sun is an enormous star. What goes on inside it? With your parents' permission, go to www.pitara.com and research how stars make their own light. What did you find out?

_____

_____

_____

Day 3: Check Within

In your investigations, you read about the stars' source of light. Even the smallest light will remove total darkness. Read Ephesians 5:8–11. Jesus Christ is the Light come into darkness. In your prayers this week, ask the Lord where you are still living in the dark; the not-so-nice things you do, say, or think. God knows you want to talk to Him. Go ahead and talk to Him now.

_____

_____

_____

Day 4: Check Around

The night sky tells us a Bible truth—the _darker_ the sky, the _brighter_ the stars (light). Read John 3:19–21. The Light (God) shows people their dark side, the wrong they do. It is tough to talk to kids about God's Light, because they do not want to admit they are doing wrong. How might you help that special friend see the dark or wrong thing(s) they are doing?

_____

_____

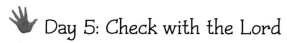 # Day 5: Check with the Lord

Read Psalm 24:1–2 then pray this prayer:

Thank you God for my eyes that see the stars thousands of miles away! You have placed those stars with all their shininess there to remind me of You. The Bible says You are the Light come down from heaven, Jesus. I want my faith to be an example to kids in my school and my family. I need Your strength when I am so tired, Your love when no one cares, and powerful words to encourage myself and others. Please remind me of the kids I am to pray for. In Jesus's name I pray, Amen.

Week 41
The Ocean's Jellies

"Hey can you see me? Can you? I'm over here! Oh well." Those words could be the words of two people in the pitch dark who cannot find one another. But now, think deep, really deep. Way down in the ocean, just about any ocean in the world, you might hear these words if a luminescent jellyfish could talk or even think.

Before the dinosaurs walked the earth, "jellies" have continued to pulse along ocean currents. They travel in large groups or blooms (even up to 100,000!), because the ocean currents keep them together[1]. Cnidarians are a group of animals to which jellyfish belong. There are thousands of species and all are made of about 95-percent water[2]. God created each one very colorful with awesome pinks, yellows, blues, purples and luminescent (or almost invisible). The jelly fishes' bright colors might seem to work against a long life where there are many predators lurking. But instead, the colors warn their enemies to stop short of going after a dangerous jelly for dinner. From the size of a grape to as large as an 8-foot (2.438 m) table, all jellyfish come with the same body parts to help them survive[3].

Having no skeleton, no head, no brain, and no central nervous system, these fancy-looking critters depend on their poisonous tentacles for catching prey, defending themselves, and quick bursts of speed. Jellyfish travel by contracting and relaxing the muscles on the outer edge of their bell or umbrella. Just like an umbrella opens and shuts, so do the muscles of its bell. When its bell opens up, water comes in and then when it closes, water propels this cool-looking creature forward. A jellyfish can have just a few to over several hundred poisonous tentacles dangling from its mouth area depending on the size of it. When prey swims by, the poisonous tip of its tentacle touches the prey paralyzing it. Once they've paralyzed their prey, the jellyfish can begin their feast[4].

What about You?

Beautiful and yet very dangerous, jellyfish can fool a person who does not know how dangerous they are. Like jellyfish can fool you, they aren't the only surprises in our world; just about anything in our world can take you by surprise. Like a movie that looks cool in the advertisement yet is really scary or full of bad language. The box of a computer game might look cool, but all that cool stuff is really violence or adult materials in the game.

Before you know it, you might be swept away in the "poisonous tentacles" of an exciting game or program that may lead to dangerous or upsetting outcomes. The Lord Jesus shows you a way of escape before it is too late. Do you have the Lord Jesus inside your heart? The Holy Spirit gives you direction, cautions you, and gives you encouragement. Listen for that whisper. Find today's scripture verse in your Bible and underline it.

Those who trust their own insight are foolish, but
anyone who walks in wisdom is safe.
Proverbs 28:26 NLT

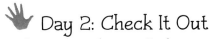

Day 2: Check It Out

Jellyfish have not changed much since God created them. These guys do not need blood or bones. They also have strange bodies that eat and expel waste from one opening[5]. With your parents' permission, search on YouTube for "Australia's Box jellyfish: Most Venomous Animal in the World." What did you find out?

_____

_____

_____

Day 3: Check Within

There are thousands of species or kinds of jellies[6]. Each species has a little something different than the next, but they are all jellies. Read 1 Corinthians 12:12–27. Each Christian kid has a different gift or way to help God. But what does verse 13 say all Christians have in common?

_____

_____

_____

Day 4: Check Around

Make sure you know what a jelly looks like so you can avoid being stung by any part of its body. Like the jellyfish can fool many people, kids can believe they are going to heaven when they don't believe Jesus Christ is both God and the Son of the living God. Read John 14:6 and Luke 21:8. How does the Bible say you can make sure you are heaven bound? How might you prepare your mind to help kids with any confusion they have about God?

_____

_____

_____

Day 5: Check with the Lord

Pray this prayer:

Dear God, jellyfish are very strange and it is hard to understand how they can live with so many weird yet awesome body parts. But You created those animals with Your hands! They all remind me that the strange things of this world that confuse me are seen by You, and somehow You are in control of it all! Help me, God, not to judge kids for their different beliefs, but instead show me how to be Your hands and feet so I can show them Your love. In Jesus's name I pray, Amen.

Write your own short prayer asking God to help you remember to sit in quietness each day with your Bible and devotional.

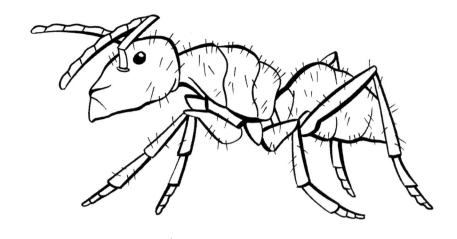

Week 42
Tiny Titans

Fire ants come out of their long winter sleep with a few things on their to-do list—make a nest underground and make it as big as possible. Anything that gets in the way will get stung. These aggressive insects first came to North America from South America in the early 1920s on cargo ships. Ships used soil for balancing the cargo in those days. Some of those ships had some aggressive, tiny stow-a-ways on board. The ants colonized while in the heap of soil, so when the ships came into port, the fire ants found their way to the ground and soon mixed with the calmer, native ants becoming a fierce species[1]. As of today, researchers say fire ants have made colonies on over 300,000,000 acres (1,214,056.92 square km) nationwide. And it keeps growing. Why? America does not have the natural enemies of the fire ant like South America does[2].

These tiny titans do not have a problem with focus. They are focused and very organized tunnel diggers, guard troops, winged male and female breeders, foragers, and queens. Tunnel diggers dig new hallways as the troops grow from the tiny eggs that are in egg rooms. The guard fire ants stay near the doorway of the mound waiting to feel vibrations and then attack their enemies with bites. The foragers look for food, and the queen keeps laying eggs.

When a person steps on one of their fortified mounds, which in some cases can contain more than five hundred thousand ants, the vibrations bring the furious guard ants to attack. Within seconds, the reddish-brown to black-colored ants will sting with painful, fiery venom. The ant will grip the skin with its jaws and begin to sting in a circle pattern. The same ant will continue releasing a chemical into the body of its victim called histamine. This is what causes the pain, itching, swelling, and redness in people's reactions to bites.[3].

What about You?

If you have ever had one of the nasty fire ant's bites, more than likely you now keep a heads-up alert when walking barefoot in the summer. Fire ants will strike at anyone's feet or body part. Like fire ants that give nasty bites, the world can also be nasty sometimes to you.

When you least expect it, just like a fire ant bite, your happy day can turn sad by something or someone. It happens so fast, and it seems you have no time to think of how to handle the hurt it has caused you. But if you know Jesus as your Savior, He wants you to tell Him about your bad day. Find today's scripture verses in your Bible and underline them.

Give all your worries and cares to God, for he cares about you. Stay alert! Watch out for your great enemy, the devil. Stand firm against him, and be strong in your faith.
1 Peter 5:7, 9 NLT

Day 2: Check It Out

Joke Question: What is the most celebrated holiday on the fire ant calendar? Answer: Mother's Day! With your parents' permission, visit the library or go online to find out what a fire ant mound looks like. The queen fire ant is very busy with eggs. Just how many eggs in its lifetime does a single queen get credit for on fire ant mothers' day? What did you find out?

_____

_____

_____

🖐 Day 3: Check Within

With the first sting, a fire ant releases an "alarm" chemical which excites more ants to sting[4]. These nasty insects gain victory by being a ready-set army. Read Ephesians 6:12–18. What does verse 12 mean? This war is invisible and ongoing. Who is the Christians' *full* armor?

_____

_____

_____

🖐 Day 4: Check Around

Fire ants' main power is in their sting. The main power within Jesus Christ is God's unconditional love. Kids do not hear enough about God's love, the kind of love that loves them no matter who they are or what they have done. Who do you know that is disabled or maybe is upset about their family? Ask Jesus to show you how to give God's love to them.

_____

_____

_____

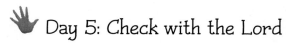 ## Day 5: Check with the Lord

Read Psalm 97:10, and then pray this prayer:

Dear Lord, the fire ants do so much damage to the earth and most of it is underground where we can't see. The spiritual battles fought in the heavens are invisible, but You can see, and You have won those battles already. Kids all over my school have problems, but You know all about them. I want them to know You, Jesus. Help them to find You in each tough thing that happens to them. Please give them a desire to find out more about You. Let me be that one to help them with their questions about You. Help me to find a new friend at my school who also loves You. In Jesus's name I pray, Amen.

Week 43
What Was That? A Bird or a Bee

You know springtime is around the corner when you see the tiny, color-ful, and speedy hummingbird. These little guys look and sound more like big bees than birds. There are over three hundred species of humming-birds living in Central and South America, with only about sixteen spe-cies breeding in North America[1]. The "hummers'" long, pointed beak, iridescent (shiny) feathers, and about eighty wing flaps per second make these little "helicopters" the coolest thing to check out on a hot summers day.

This summer, look for a big patch of flowers and stand by them very still and quietly. A 60 mph [2] (96.56 kph) blur with a loud hum might come screeching to a halt right in front of your face. As the hummer hov-ers in mid-air, its tiny but mighty wings make a loud vibrating noise as its eyes seem to study you. It can totally freak you out. The stealth body of a hummer uses roughly 30 percent of its muscle just for flying.

The country of Cuba is where the smallest of hummingbirds live. Weighing only .05 ounces (1.4g)[3], the bee hummingbird finds the top of a pencil eraser a comfortable roost. Over and over again, it is mistaken for a bee, when of course it is a bird. Bee hummers are the smallest warm-blooded vertebra (critter with a backbone)[4]. With no fat around its bones to keep it from loosing body heat, God gave the wisp of a bird a fast metabolism. During normal flying, its metabolism is so high because its heart beats 1,200 times a minute. At times, the hummer can slow down its own rate at which it burns calories. And so the hummers need to eat, eat, and eat some more to keep their finely tuned machine of a body going strong[5]. How does eating half your weight in bugs each day and eight times your weight in nectar or sugar water sound? That is the daily menu for hummingbirds. God's design for this awesome creature is another clue to His remarkable plan for all His creation.

What about You?

Hummingbirds are itty, bitty creatures. Their little bodies have to work so hard, and they have to always be eating so they can keep flying. Its smallness and need for food all the time would appear to be its defeat. It seems that after all these thousands of years on earth they would have died off like dinosaurs. But, in fact, the hummingbird is a champ.

When you believe your every worry, every fear, and every single problem is understood by the Lord in His heart, then you are a champion too. That belief gives you stamina like the hummers to go through every day, but it is called "power from on high." That power comes from within you if you know Jesus. You need to go to Jesus in prayer and quiet time to get re-fueled each day. Ask God to make some scripture personalized, to make them count special for your life. He will when you ask! Find today's scripture verse in your Bible and underline it.

The Lord God is my strength. He makes me like a deer that
does not stumble so I can walk on the steep mountains.
Habakkuk 3:19 NCV

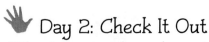 Day 2: Check It Out

Joke Question: What is smarter than a hummingbird? Answer: A spelling bee! Hummingbirds are like tiny helicopters because they fly up, down, backward, and sideways, and even upside down. With your parents' permission, visit the library or go online to find out why the hummer can fly in so many directions. What is different about its wings compared to other birds? What did you find out?

_____

_____

_____

✋ Day 3: Check Within

What activity do you see hummingbirds doing most of the time? Hummers might be tiny but they are very busy pollinating flowers, and guess what? They do not let bigger and stronger birds bully them. Read 1 Timothy 4:12. Instead of thinking that you are too young or God can't use you, what does the scripture say you should do?

_____

_____

_____

✋ Day 4: Check Around

Hummingbirds are created with a body that needs consistent fuel so they can power through their day. Read 2 Timothy 3:16. According to this scripture, how is the Word of God for you like sugar water is to the hummer? What recent scripture have you found helpful in understanding your family or friends?

_____

187

_____

_____

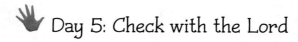 Day 5: Check with the Lord

Pray this prayer:

Lord God, like the hummer needs sugar, I need You to whisper to me that I am a child of the King when some kids hurt my feelings. I will never stop being thankful that You hear my softest cry for help when no one else hears me. I need You to hear my confession when I say mean things to kids. And I know You will hear and smile when I come to You in prayer and confession. Thank You for forgiving me so long ago on the cross. Show me how to love today like You love me every day. In Jesus's name I pray, Amen.

Write your own short prayer letting God know how thankful you are because He loves you in spite of your mess ups.

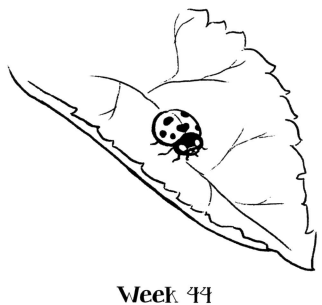

Week 44
Aphid Lions

What if you could fly? Fly way up with the wind, birds, and the bugs? You might run into a backward-flying bug. The ladybug (or ladybird) can lift off a plant and then fly backward when it wants[1]. This tiny red-and-black beetle is in the Coleoptera family of beetles. Coleoptera is a Greek word which means "sheath-winged." There are about 350,000–400,000 species [2] of beetles, and the ladybugs number about 5,000–6,000 different species [3] within the Coeoptera family. Insects are the largest group of animals on the earth, and beetles are the largest family inside the insect group[4].

Ladybugs are like the panda bear of the insect world, because they are loved by everyone, including farmers. Farmers are really into ladybugs. Why? Aphids are not liked by farmers. Aphids are insects like the ladybug, but they eat what the farmers are trying to grow. Ladybugs eat the aphids that eat and ruin the farmers' crops and gardeners' plants. A long time ago, farmers found the eating habits of ladybugs to be very important. They realized ladybugs to be a much cheaper and safer way than chemicals to save their crops from complete ruin. If a farmer uses enough of the little aphid-eating insect, he will be able to raise healthy plants which can then be shipped off to stores for people to eat[5].

Hanging out in a farmer's field of crops is like sitting down to the best aphid buffet for the ladybug. One ladybug can chow down an aphid in no time at all. The adult will gobble up about fifty-sixty[6] aphids in a day, and in its short life cycle (three to six weeks) about 5,000[7] aphids will be munched up and eaten by a single ladybug beetle. Is God not amazing as He plans even the little bellies of bugs? So, the ladybug is much more than just a cute, little beetle with spots. The Lord gave this critter a lion of an appetite for aphids. He might as well be nick-named the aphid lion.

What about You?

Just knowing the ladybugs are serious eaters gives a farmer peace of mind. These itty-bitty creations of God do not, of course, know how useful they are. When the Lord created this tiny beetle, He had jobs already for it to do. The insect has value to both God and to farmers and gardeners.

Like the beetle, you may not even know how important you are in the life of a friend or even just a kid you do not know at school. The Lord wants you to *know* His son Jesus. Jesus can show you all the ways you can be a special friend to someone like the beetle is to the farmer. It is awesome knowing you are really making a good difference in someone's life just by being you. Find today's scripture verses in your Bible and underline them.

All a man's ways seem right in his own eyes, but the Lord weighs the motives. Commit your activities to the Lord and your plans will be achieved.
Proverbs 16: 2–3 HCSB

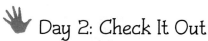 Day 2: Check It Out

Being in the family of arthropods, ladybugs have a skeleton on the outside of their bodies[8]. With your parents' permission, visit the library or go online to find just which continents have insects. How many of the seven continents have arthropods? The oceans have insects but they are called crustaceans. List some crustaceans.

🖐 Day 3: Check Within

Aphids are a true enemy of the farmer. But with the ladybug coming to his rescue, he may not have as many sleepless nights. From the Old Testament, read Lamentations 3:22–23. Though the farmer may or may not have 100-percent aphid relief, what does the book of Lamentations say about God's unchanging faithfulness for you and the farmer?

🖐 Day 4: Check Around

A mega-team of ladybugs will make the aphids just a bad memory to the farmer. Read Ecclesiastes 4:9. A friend that loves Jesus can be like a mega-teammate. The Bible says two are better than one. Who is your good friend? How can you make time for your friend?

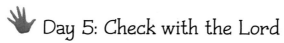

Day 5: Check with the Lord

Read Psalm 18:30, and then pray this prayer:

Dear Lord God, You are bigger than the universe, yet the Bible tells me You are my friend, too. Thank you, Lord, that even though I mess up and get myself in trouble, You are faithful to love me as if I have never messed up. That is too amazing for me to understand. I am comforted when I think about how You made and know of each of the millions of insects running all over the earth because if they are important I must be extremely valuable to You. I am a child of the Most High God! In Jesus's name I pray, Amen.

Week 45
God's Masterpieces

Some look like fancy oak leaves, some look like beautiful dinner plates, and still others look as dainty as lace. If your winters are snowy and icy, then you have seen God's masterpieces—snowflakes. But there are many who have yet to see a snowflake! Have you ever been snowboarding, hit a big bump, and face planted in the snow? The snow you just got a mouthful of was probably packed tightly, but it was made up of thousands of wonderfully unique snowflakes.

Snowflakes are not easy to come by. Temperature, wetness in the air, and the way air travels all need to be just right for the ice crystal to begin to be made. Each snowflake begins as a dust bit[1]. If the temperature is cold enough then the water vapor will begin to stick to the dust[2]. Ice crystals form when the temperature in the cloud is as low as 5°F (-15°C). As the ice crystals move up or down inside the cloud, they keep on forming and shaping into snowflakes. Soon, the flakes are heavy enough to begin to fall from the clouds[3]. No one but God knows the number of millions upon millions of snowflake patterns. Some snowflakes are six-sided hexagonal crystals that look like dinner-plate flakes and are formed in high clouds, needle-shaped flakes fall from middle clouds, and many, other six-sided shapes are formed in low clouds. The colder the temperature is, the sharper the points on each[4].

It is possible, but not probable, for two snowflakes to look alike (though they did not begin alike) when they finally land in your hand because of all the changes they go through on their way down from the clouds[5]. But no matter which shape, the snowflake is a masterpiece causing us to wonder and smile with the Creator of all the heavens and earth.

What about You?

When you are outside where it snows in winter, you do not have to go far to see God's masterpieces. Each snowflake is so unlike the next. Each can remind you of how different the Lord has designed you. Every detail of your mind, body, and personality are the handiwork of God the Father. The Bible says God *knit* you together. When they're knitting, knitters lovingly decide and create their artwork just the way they want to make them.

When we praise God, we are telling Him how good He is just because He is God. To think how God created you is an awesome thought. Give God a shout of praise for creating you just the way you are. How many parts of your body can you bow your head and thank Him for? How about a smart mind and eyes to read this page! When Jesus lives inside your heart, you want to sing and make a joyful noise to Him. Find today's scripture verses in your Bible and underline them.

You made all the delicate, inner parts of my body and knit me together in my mother's womb. You watched me as I was being formed in utter seclusion. Every moment was laid out before a single day had passed.
Psalm 139: 13, 15a, 16b, NLT

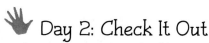 Day 2: Check It Out

With your parents' permission, visit the library or go online to find the many shapes of snowflakes. http://bentley.sciencebuff.org/ See what

Wilson Bentley (an American farmer) has to show you about these masterpieces of God. What did you find out?

_____

_____

_____

✋ Day 3: Check Within

Read and think about Matthew 16: 13–16. Jesus knew who He was. His disciple, Peter (when asked by Jesus) said "You are the Christ, the Son of the living God." What makes Jesus Christ different than John the Baptist or a prophet or any other religious figure?

_____

_____

_____

✋ Day 4: Check Around

Read John 20: 24–29. Before Thomas believed that Jesus was his Lord and God, he did not believe. There are so many kids and adults that think Jesus Christ has not risen from the dead or that He is not God. Read 2 Timothy 3:16. Where does it say you can point your friends so they can find out how different Jesus is from all other beliefs?

_____

_____

_____

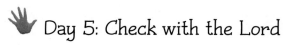

Day 5: Check with the Lord

Pray this prayer:

Lord, You are perfect and Your Word tells us that You make all things beautiful in Your time. I know that means me! I know though I am young and so small compared to the world and all You do, that You have me on Your mind! Those snowflakes remind me over and over that You are involved in the small things! You say in the Bible, "I am the way, the truth and the light, no one comes to the Father but through me." Thank You God for loving me so much and for showing me this verse that is like the key to heaven! In Jesus's name I pray. Amen.

Write your own short prayer asking God to remove any doubt you may have about Jesus, who God says is God and His only son and Savior to the world. Tell Him whatever else is in your mind.

Week 46
Dumbo Octopus

The creatures hanging out in some of the deepest parts of the oceans, like the Grimpoteuthis, or Dumbo octopus, need especially strong bodies to live within their environment. This Dumbo octopus gets it name because of the ear-like fins coming out of their heads like Disney's Dumbo. It lives deep down (in all the oceans) between 1,300–22,965 feet (400–7,000 meters). Some Dumbos are eight inches (20.32 cm) long, while still others are a whopping 6 feet long (1.83 m). These little octopods (called so because they have eight arms) will crawl on the ocean floor in search of their menu goodies. But most of the time, they drift with their eight arms stretched out, close to the bottom of their part of the ocean. The Dumbo octopus scoots through the ocean by expanding and contracting its eight arms. When they want to go faster they scoot around by flapping their Dumbo-like fins and shooting water through their funnel. Either of these methods of movement has made it victorious in the pitch-dark depths of the oceans. Being a little octopod is a blessing because their predators do not see them as well as they do other larger prey. Great escapes, by whichever method the Dumbo chooses, are easier when you are a little guy in a big ocean.

Predators have to act quickly because Dumbos will shoot their bodies like a bullet around their territories until they reach a rock crevice to hide out in. Then, when it sees prey, the Dumbo will use a few of its arms which are equipped with special harpoon-like hooks, and pull the prey into its mouth. Worms, bivalves, and other crustaceans (animals like insects that have a skeleton on the outside of their bodies and live in the water) are snacks for this little bit of energy racing through the dark abyss[1]. Do you think God sees this little creature? What might the Bible say about that?

What about You?

The Bible says, "So God created the large sea animals and every living thing that moves in the sea. The sea is filled with these living things, with each one producing more of its own kind." (Genesis1:21). The Dumbo octopus is a creation of the Lord's hand because He *thought* to create it. Even the little fins that look like Dumbo ears were made by the God who knows you.

Sometimes, do you feel invisible? Maybe you think your friends do not care when you are right there with them? The Lord sees you like He sees the tiny Dumbo octopus and all the stuff that bothers you. Jesus, the One who suffered for our sins, knows when you are really bothered with something.

What might seem dark and upsetting right now, Jesus Christ has already seen, and He can make your bad situation into a good thing. Ask Him now to help you with your friends and then wait and see how your prayer will be answered. Be sure to thank God for how He works things for your good. Find today's scripture verse and underline it in your Bible.

Search me, O God, and know my heart, test
me and know my anxious thoughts.
Psalm 139: 23 NLT

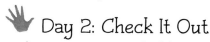

Day 2: Check It Out

With your parents' permission, visit the library or go online: www. kids-fun-science.com/challenger-deep.html. What life forms live in the deepest and darkest part of the ocean—the Challenger Deep[2]. Where is the Challenger Deep? How deep is it? Has anyone been able to study the Challenger Deep? What did you find out?

_____

_____

_____

Day 3: Check Within

Sin keeps us from God. But like the Lord sees the Dumbo octopus, the Lord sees our sin even as we try to hide it. Read Ephesians 2:4–5. But God's Son, Jesus Christ, took on your sin, died on a cross, was buried, and was raised to live forever. What does "it is by grace you have been saved" mean to you?

_____

_____

_____

Day 4: Check Around

Good news—the Lord Jesus has given new life to you or anyone, but you need to trust or receive the Good News. Read John 8: 12. The Bible says Jesus is the Light of the world. He says whoever follows Jesus will not walk in darkness. What does "not walk in darkness" mean to you? Who in your circle of friends needs God's protection and God Himself?

_____

_____

_____

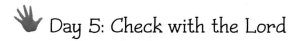 Day 5: Check with the Lord

Read Psalm 18:1–2, and then pray this prayer:

Lord God, I thank You and praise You because You are Holy and the King of kings. You see me and all my faults and still love me just as I am! Thank You for sending Your Son, the Light of the world, to bring me salvation. You alone can heal my hurts, sicknesses, and my families and friends as well. You also give me more grace or love to accept the things that don't change. I do not have to be afraid of the darkness or kids that hurt my feelings, I just need to bring it all to You. You know when I am anxious, and so I will wait for You to bring me peace once again. Thank You, God, for sending your angels to keep watch over me! In Jesus's name I pray, Amen.

Week 47
Venus Flytrap

In the wetlands of the Carolinas lives a meat-eating plant, the Venus flytrap. Like any other plant God makes, this plant needs nutrients and minerals from the soil. But the wetlands do not supply enough nutrients the flytrap needs so the insects make this curious plant healthier. Each Venus flytrap is made up of two hinges or leaves that are green on the outside and red on the inside, a few trigger hairs, a sweet flower smell, and energy to open and shut its traps. The traps stay open (unless it is digesting) so that the bugs and flies can be attracted to the red parts and the plant's sweet smell.

The Venus flytrap is a plant that invites and then traps insects. These meat-eating plants eat all sorts of insects—ants, flies, worms, crickets, and spiders. The sweet smell makes an ant or a worm crawl up into the leaves or a fly to land on its traps. Then the tiny trigger hairs that are on the red part will sense movement causing the two traps or leaves to zap shut in less than one second. As the bug wriggles around trying to free itself, the trap tightens, leaving no way of escape, and soon the digestive enzymes (much like our stomach enzymes) begin to be released by the plant. Within a week or so, the flytrap's digestive juices dissolve the tiny bug parts absorbing them back into its leaves. The harder shells of insects are blown away by the wind or rain. When the plant is finished, its leaves will open again and the sweet wisps of flower fragrance will begin to attract another innocent insect[1].

What about You?

Once a little critter steps onto the sweet-smelling red leaf his life is over. The trap is set, and the bait looks so good to the insect. But what looks good, leads to the bug's death. God's word tells Christians to be careful who we hang out with, where we take ourselves, what we listen to every day.

Reading your Bible every day, talking to God, and hanging out with others who love God are super ways to stay away from "traps" or bad situations. One trap might be a movie that looks really good, but your parents have told you no, knowing it might influence you in the wrong way. The friends you have might be fun, but what are they into? Ask the Lord Jesus to keep you from the wrong kinds of things, places, and people. He always wants what is best for His children. Find today's scripture verses in your Bible and underline them.

I have taught you the way of wisdom. I have guided you along decent paths. Guard your heart more than anything else, because the source of your life flows from it.
Proverbs 4:11, 23 GWT

Day 2: Check It Out

Venus flytraps are carnivorous plants, which means they receive some or most of their nutrients from trapping and ingesting animals. With your parents' permission, visit the library or go online to find a few more carnivorous plants. There are five basic trapping-kinds of plants. What did you find out? If you have some time, ask your parents to take you to a plant nursery where you can see the flytraps.

_____

_____

_____

🖐 Day 3: Check Within

Venus flytraps might seem like they do no good because they trap and digest their victims. But the flytrap is only doing what it needs to do to survive. It is what it is! Read Romans 3:9–12. How many people are righteous? The Bible says "there is no one who does good." What do you think God means by "good"?

_____

_____

_____

🖐 Day 4: Check Around

God does not judge plants as good or bad. But He does judge people according to His own goodness. God has made a way for people who do bad things as well as good things to be accepted by Himself. The good things you do will not get you to heaven! Read Romans 3:22 and Ephesians 2:8–9. What does grace mean? How does it say a person may be made right or righteous for God?

_____

_____

_____

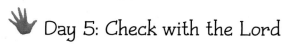

Day 5: Check with the Lord

Pray this prayer:

Lord God, there is always something that surprises me when I study all the cool animals and plants. Genesis 1:25 says that after You created animals, You said, "And God saw that it was good." All the good things I do for You and anyone else does not get me into heaven! So many kids don't know that. You are so good, Lord. Thank You for showing me that no one and no thing is able to be right or good on their own. If I did not read this, how would I have realized that I needed to be right and that Jesus Christ is my only Righteousness? In Jesus's name I pray, Amen.

Write your own short prayer thanking God for sending Jesus to die on the cross for your sin so that you could go to heaven one day.

Week 48
Hotdogs with an Attitude

Naked mole rats, or sand puppies as the Africans call them, are mammals which live underground all the time, making tunnels and a whole world in which to live. They look like hotdogs (about 3 inches long, or 7.6 cm) with tiny eyes, only about a hundred strands of hair around their bodies, and teeth that are a dentist's worst nightmare. Like ants or termites or wasps, the naked mole rats live in a caste system where animals live and work in a ranking order for the purpose of keeping alive.

The ruling queen rat is the drill sergeant of the caste. She lives to have babies and directs all the naked mole rats in her colony. During her pregnancies, her tiny backbone grows, allowing for her three-inch-long body to carry twelve to twenty-seven pups. In one year, she can deliver up to five litters. No wonder she is the queen "bee." Just under the queen's rank are a few breeding males. Under them, are the soldiers who do the guard duty. Male and female soldiers are always a ready-to-go swat team whenever alien mole rats or other enemies threaten. God has equipped these hotdog-looking creatures with a set of tools (teeth) just *outside* their mouth that never become dull and never stop growing. The workers who are last on the rank do the tunneling with these sharp teeth, and the few hairs they have act like sensors keeping each worker aware of how close things are. Digging extensive tunnels and seeking out their favorite food and roots, are on the workers to-do list to keep the queen happy.

God gave the naked mole rat a slow metabolism—not even half that of a mouse. There is always a reason why God does things. Having this slow metabolism causes animals not to breathe as often as other animals. This metabolism makes living underground easy work for them because there is not much oxygen underground. Their tiny eyes are almost blind[1]. Why would they need big eyes in the pitch dark?

What about You?

Sand puppies can live up to twenty-seven years. Under the ground and under your shoes where no one sees, these critters do their jobs day in and day out. These blind and determined critters do not get bored, do not quit doing their jobs, and do not get tired of the dark. Why? Because God made them just the way they are.

The Bible says God makes no mistakes. Do you know anyone like these mole rats? A kid that works hard, does not complain, yet goes unnoticed? Maybe they do not have a friend at school. Maybe they are embarrassed of their clothes or maybe they are disabled and feel self-conscious. Why not bring some light into a kid's day tomorrow with some nice words or maybe an invitation to hang out. We all like those invites! Find today's scripture verse in your Bible and underline it.

The right word spoken at the right times is as beautiful as gold apples in a silver bowl.
Proverbs 25:11 NCV

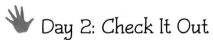 Day 2: Check It Out

Living underground can pose some pretty tough problems. Can you guess which of the naked mole rat's senses are more developed than others? With your parents' permission, visit the library or go online to find the mole rats stronger senses and why they need them. What did you find out?

_____

_____

_____

🖐 Day 3: Check Within

In the mole rat colony there seems to be no room for mistakes or displeasing the queen. Do you feel like you keep making mistakes? Are you afraid to even make a mistake? Read Psalm 103:8–14. What does it say? Make a list of what God says about your mistakes. How does this list surprise you?

_____

_____

_____

🖐 Day 4: Check Around

The naked mole rat has everything it needs, so it really does not have much waiting to do. Waiting to get things or waiting for things to happen can make you anxious and ruin a good day. Read Lamentations 3:24–26. This is a good verse to memorize. How can you help a friend or family member after reading this verse?

_____

_____

_____

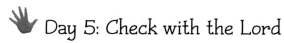

Day 5: Check with the Lord

Read Psalm 56:3–4, and then pray this prayer:

Lord God, I am waiting for You this morning. So many times I want to do things my own way. Then I keep hiding the mistakes I make. I don't want to hide them. I want to tell You about everything I have inside. The Bible says I can come and just sit by myself and cry out to You. You already died for my sin and forgave me. I want to keep my heart aware that You are with me; then I will have a peaceful heart once again! I am so thankful that You do not hide from me like the naked mole rat that is hidden underground. In Jesus's name I pray, Amen.

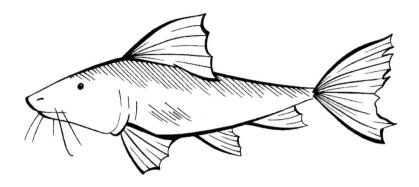

Week 49
The Big and Mighty Amazon

Humongous, gargantuan, colossal, gigantic, and mammoth are awesome words people use to describe the Amazon River in South America. Now you need to get out your map of the world. With your finger, slowly trace the path of the Amazon River.

The gigantic Amazon River starts its trek from Peru then goes into Ecuador, Venezuela, Bolivia, Colombia, Guyana, and ends in Brazil. Depending on who you talk to, the river is between 3,903 miles (6,281 km) long and 4,195 miles (6,751 km) long—wider than the United States from coast to coast. The Amazon River carries more fresh water than any other river on God's earth. During the wet or rainy season, the river can be up to some 25 miles (40.2 km) wide. Amazingly, the Amazon carries one-fifth or 20 percent of the fresh or non-salt water that flows into the earth's oceans[1]. When it arrives on the coast of Brazil, the mouth of the river is some 202 miles (325 km) wide in the rainy season. At the mouth, the powerful fresh waters mix with the salt water of the Atlantic Ocean making it less salty for some 200 miles (321 km) out into the ocean. Being so wide and deep at its mouth, ocean-going ships can travel its waters as far up the river as two-thirds of the whole length of the Amazon[2].

This humongous river is also home to its own extreme creatures unlike any others on earth. Catfish are usually eight inches to five feet long and weigh up to 60 pounds (27.22 kg). Not so in the gargantuan Amazon. How about catfish weighing over 200 lbs. (90.7 kg)? This great river is also the home of the largest freshwater fish, the Arapaima gigas or Pirarucu, which can weigh up to 440 lbs. (199 kg).[3]

What about You?

No doubt about it, everything is bigger than big when it comes to describing the Amazon River. Even one of the world's largest snakes, the Anaconda, lurks in the shallow waters of the Amazon Basin[4]. And guess what? The Lord God filled that river and created all the animals that continue to live and grow in it!

The Amazon has nothing about it that is small. Your life is like the Amazon to God. He sees your life as a big part of His. Jesus said, "I have come that you might have life and have it full." Have you asked Jesus to give you a full life to live every day? What does it mean to live your daily life "full"? Maybe it means letting God take charge. He will surprise you when you ask Him what a full life can mean to you. Find today's scripture in your Bible and underline it.

Ask me and I will tell you remarkable secrets you
do not know about things to come.
Jeremiah 33:3 NIV

Day 2: Check It Out

The Amazon is one of the largest rivers in the world. In 1991, the STS-43 space mission took pictures of the Amazon River from space. Their photos amazed the world[5]. With your parents' permission, visit the library or online. Look at the Amazon River pictures on www.

universetoday.com. Check out the awesome images on the NASA web-site. www.nasa.gov/audience/forstudents/index.html. What did you see?

_____

_____

_____

🖐 Day 3: Check Within

When you read about the Amazon River and see the cool images shot from space you cannot help but feel so small. But are you small to God? Read Daniel 10:12–14. Your prayers go straight to God but only in His perfect timing. The scripture says there are powerful battles being fought in the heavens between God's angels and Satan's. How many weeks did Daniel wait to hear from God? What did he keep doing? What have you been talking to God that is taking so long?

_____

_____

_____

🖐 Day 4: Check Around

At the mouth of the Amazon, about eight trillion gallons (35,239,070,399 cubic meters) of water are powerfully discharged each day into the Atlantic[6]. Praying with other people that love God is power-ful. Read Acts 12:5–11. Why do you think Peter escape so miraculously? How has the Lord answered one of your prayers about a friend with such power?

_____

_____

_____

 ## Day 5: Check with the Lord

Pray this prayer:

Dear Lord, You are always busy doing good because You are good twenty-four-seven all the time. At bedtime, I close my eyes to go to sleep, and I have peace because You know me and all my needs, fear, worries, and secrets. How awesome You are! You send Your angels to watch over me both day and night. I do not have to ask, "Do You hear me?" Help me be a good friend, one that is sad when my friend is sad. I want to get excited when my friend shares good news. I want to remember to pray each night for my friends. In Jesus's name I pray, Amen.

Write your own short prayer telling the Lord about your friend's need, asking God to help them.

Week 50
Nothing Is Hidden from God

Horses are strong and speedy animals. There are many horses with winning titles to their names. But there is one sort of horse that is quite different. How about the horse that has no legs, is forever slow, has no voice, and is so small you could stuff it in your pocket?

Clinging to a piece of sea grass with his long prehensile tail, the male seahorse is about to give birth. What? Carrying the eggs and giving birth to them is what the dads do in the seahorse households. Dad has a pouch like a kangaroo and mom puts her minute eggs inside the pouch. In forty to sixty days, two hundred to six hundred baby seahorses spout really fast from the dad's pouch. This dad can be in labor (having babies) for up to three days. They pop up to the surface of the water immediately to fill their tiny swim bladder (like a human's lung) with air. This air-filled, swim bladder needs to balance the seahorse as it lives upright under the water. So far, scientists have not found another animal group anywhere on earth where the dad gives birth to the babies[1]. Seahorses of all kinds are God's surprises to us. Just when we think we know a ton of things about animals, the Lord uncovers new things to show us.

The thirty-five species of Seahorses live in oceans, hanging out amongst sea grasses and coral. Their bodies camouflage well so they will not get on someone's lunch menu. Our Creator has given them special tails (prehensile) that curl up around sea grasses and corals to keep them anchored from the ocean currents and safely hidden from predators while they eat up to three thousand tiny microscopic animals a day. Without a stomach, they have to constantly be eating to keep their energy. Even though they are not speedy critters, their dorsal fin beats a crazy thirty-five times a second as they slowly maneuver around the sea grasses. God has his eye even on this petite fish wanting for its safety. He wrapped them in armor-type, bony plates with sharp points acting in their defense when touched[2]. Seahorses are an awesome little animal to see.

What about You?

No matter how small or large, whether hidden away or big as an elephant, God thought about it before He created it! He has created the seahorse to live its life right in the very place it lives. Every part of the seahorse's life makes you think how incredible God is as the only Creator of life. He keeps the seahorse alive deep down where no one really thinks about! That is very cool for you to think about today. Psalm 119:73a says, "You made me and formed me with your hands."

Just like the seahorse dads keep their tiny tails wrapped or anchored around sea grass during the birthing process, you too can know Jesus has a mighty hand on you. When you accept Jesus as your Savior, He can be like an anchor helping you to hang around with the right kids and being the One you bring your concerns to. Find today's scripture verse in your Bible and underline it.

The Lord will work out His plans for my life—
for your faithful love endures forever.
Psalm 138:8a NLT

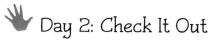

Day 2: Check It Out

Everything is miniscule about this critter. The seahorse's tiny eyes work independently of one another[3]. With your parents' permission, visit the library or go online to discover more about why the seahorses have independently working eyes. What reptile can you think of that has the same independently working eyes? Try to draw the awesomely camouflaged Leafy seahorse or the Big Belly seahorses. What did you find out?

_____

_____

_____

Day 3: Check Within

Little seahorses have a unique experience because their father gives birth to them. Being a parent means sacrificing or giving up your own needs and wants in order to love and raise your child. Read John 3:16–17. God is the ultimate Father. He is God. He gave the greatest sacrifice ever. What was the sacrifice? How does His sacrifice affect you?

_____

_____

_____

Day 4: Check Around

The baby seahorses are so small when they are born which makes them an easy lunch bite for many predators. But God has plans for those

215

seahorses, no matter how little or small. Read 1 Samuel 3. Eli knew God had special plans for young Samuel. Do you have a friend who doesn't feel good about themselves or maybe thinks they are not important? How can you bring help to that friend?

_____

_____

_____

 ## Day 5: Check with the Lord

Read Psalm 91:1–2, and then pray this prayer:

Thank You, God, for the story of Samuel. It helps me better understand that I need to listen and then learn to know Your voice. Just like You have Your eye on the little seahorses, I know that, even though I am just a kid, You have giant plans for me today. I need to spend time with my devotional and Bible. Please help me to do just that, God. When I place my head on my pillow tonight, I want to remember how faithful You were to me all day. Thank You for waking me up and giving me all Your love this morning. In Jesus's name I pray, Amen.

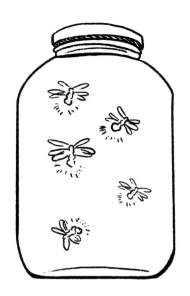

Week 51
Blink-Blink-Blink Bugs

Sitting around a toasty camp fire on a summer's night, you see sparks pop and dance off into the darkness. Suddenly you see something else. Those little bits of dancing fire seem to be and then not be. What's up? It is not fire sparks at all, but lightening bugs.

The flashing is caused by enzymes breaking down cells of crystals or chemical substances inside their bellies. This is energy set off in the form of light. It is not hot light, but in fact it is cool[1]. Blink, blink, blink are what they do to attract mates. Each species has its own fixed pattern of blinking and all for the purpose of finding a mate. It's like when you're dancing with someone; if you do not keep up with the other person, then your dance gets messed up. If a lightening bug sends out a blink in a certain pattern or code, but too late or too slow, then the whole mating opportunity is a loss for both bugs[2].

Fireflies or lightening bugs are not even flies, but beetles. There are about two thousand different sorts or species of these critters hanging out in mostly moist and warm areas around the earth. The fireflies come from two groups or families of beetle. One family is found in Europe, North America, and Australia, where they live in trees. The second is found on the Pacific Islands. Often, people will mix up lightening bugs with their cousins, the glow worms, which give off a softer light[3].

What about You?

No doubt about it, if a firefly is out and about on a summer night, we will see him with our eyes. Its light gives it away, right? Like the firefly's light is unmistakable to those around it, you too can stand out in a good way. How? If you are a Christian, you have the light of Christ living inside. He is greater than any situation, any attitude you might have, or any problem in your life. Thank God with a good attitude next time something doesn't go your way. God will give you a strangely unique peace about it. Do kids see that blink-blink light in your everyday life through your actions and reactions? Or does it go out when things do not go your way, preventing others from seeing Jesus in you? Find today's scripture verses in your Bible and underline them.

The Lord is my light and the one who saves me... During danger he
will keep me safe in his shelter. He will hide me in his Holy tent.
Psalm 27: 1,5a NCV

You are the light of the world—like a city on a hilltop that cannot be
hidden. No one lights a lamp and then puts it under a basket. Instead, a
lamp is placed on a stand, where it gives light to everyone in the house.
Matthew 5: 14 -15 NLT

Day 2: Check It Out

Fireflies are curious little beetles living in moist areas of the world. With your parents' permission, visit the library or go online (YouTube) to find out what hundreds of these critters do only once a year in Gatlinburg, Tennessee, USA. What did you find out?

_____

_____

🖐 Day 3: Check Within

Fireflies have no problem finding one another, especially at night. It's pretty hard not to recognize your buddy if you are a firefly. Read Colossians 3:12–16. These virtues are not a choice, but a direct command for Christians to do. Re-read this scripture and, with God's help, list the virtues that you think kids see in you at school and home.

_____

_____

_____

🖐 Day 4: Check Around

In the four gospels, Jesus often told stories called parables. Read the parable in Mark 4:30–32. A parable often compared one thing with another—an earthly story with a heavenly meaning. Take some time to think and then create a parable using fireflies to help kids understand how Jesus is the Light of the world.

_____

_____

_____

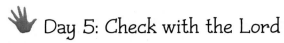 # Day 5: Check with the Lord

Pray this prayer:

Dear Lord God, today I worship You once again just because You are God. You light up little bugs, reminding me of Your imagination creating them and me. When I wake up in the morning, I want to remember You first and ask You to lead me as though we were both fireflies. Only with Your love inside me can I have the power to be in control of the words that I speak and the things I do. I love You so much. In Jesus's name I pray, Amen.

Write your own short prayer asking God to give you patience with other kids. Also, what might you pray about your attitude lately?

Week 52
We Are the Sheep of His Pasture

It will soon be Christmas. Did you remember to set up your nativity scene? If so, did you happen to notice the little sheep figurines? Sheep were a huge part of the very first Christmas Eve. The Bible tells us that God chose sheep to describe His children because people behave a lot like sheep. What is it that makes a sheep a sheep? The answer to that question might show us why sheep need a shepherd.

Sheep need a shepherd because they have many needs. While munching on grasses, sheep forget to look where they are going and can suddenly find themselves all alone up on a rocky cliff. This problem is why a sheep also needs a flock. Any wolf knows to look for sheep folds when lunchtime rolls around because there is always one little sheep that forgets. The wolf can easily draw a sheep away by stalking it and making it scared, and soon it forgets to stay with the rest of the sheep. When lost, they are helpless without one another and their shepherd. Without realizing it, a sheep can get entangled in a bush. But the shepherd knows all these things if he is a good shepherd. A good shepherd provides a healthy pasture for eating, but he also has to watch them very carefully or they can eat too much and get sick and die.

And so the sheep look to their shepherd because he tenderly cares for them. As he bathes them, the good shepherd carefully checks for eye diseases, ear ticks, body fleas, and stomach bloat. The good shepherd is alert during the night for any hungry predators, knowing his sheep are defenseless and very dependent upon him. He knows each sheep's cry, and the sheep know their shepherd's call. If one should tumble down a hillside the shepherd knows and he goes after it. How does he know, out of so many sheep, that one is missing? Because a good shepherd counts each sheep one by one making sure each one is within the sheep fold at the end of the day[1].

What about You?

Read Luke 2: 8–9. While the shepherds took care of their sheep the night Jesus was born, what does the Bible say the sheep were doing? What were the shepherds doing? Sheep do not get scared when their shepherd is close by. They feel safe so they can lie down. Without the shepherd's protection all day and all night, sheep would otherwise get scared and many would die. The Bible tells us that God's children are His sheep. If you have Jesus living inside your heart, you are one of God's precious lambs. You need God's help as well when you are scared, feel lonely, or get yourself in a mess. The Bible is God's love letter to you. Each time you read the Bible, God is showing you how deep and high He loves you!

Find today's scripture verses and underline them in your Bible.

He calls his own sheep by name and leads them out. (4) After he has gathered his own flock, he walks ahead of them, and they follow him because they know his voice. (5) They will not follow a stranger; they will run from him because they do not know his voice.
John 10: 3b, 4, 5 NLT

Day 2: Check It Out

Sheep have been called names like "stupid" or "dumb." When you find out more about sheep, you discover those names aren't right. With your parents' permission, visit the library or go online to find out the truth about sheep. One cool truth is sheep race like horses, but you have to read about it to believe it. Visit www.sheep101.info. What did you find out?

_____

_____

_____

🖐 Day 3: Check Within

The Bible says Jesus came to earth during the night, and his mother, Mary, placed Him in a manger or animal eating trough. When the sheep bleated, Jesus's little ears must have heard their cries. Jesus loves His sheep with all His heart and still hears His sheep's cries. Read John 10:2–3, 14–15 and Psalm 18:6. Ever since your first cry until this very moment, God has heard you with His ears. How does that make you feel? How can you know if you are a true sheep of the Shepherd Jesus?

_____

_____

_____

🖐 Day 4: Check Around

The Bible uses the nature of sheep and goats to describe human hearts. Sheep (Christians) follow Christ; goats (unbelievers) do not. Sheep are gentle, innocent, obedient, and quiet. Goats are rebellious. Read Matthew 25:31–33. God will separate the pretenders and the rebellious from His faithful followers. What does it mean to follow after Christ? How can you?

_____

_____

_____

 # Day 5: Check with the Lord

Pray this prayer:

Lord, Christmas Day is the most special of all days. You, God, came all the way from heaven through time and space into a little, hay-filled, animal trough in Bethlehem. The sheep and all the animals did not realize You, the Savior of the world, were with them. I try to picture that Holy night in my mind. Thank You, Jesus, that You have given me the opportunity to be one of Your sheep! The Bible says in John 10 that You hear Your sheep when they call You by name, Jesus. When Your sheep whisper Your name, You hear them. They think Your name, and You know who they are. God, You even know their thoughts before they think them. To be one of Your sheep is the best way to love You! Happy birthday, Jesus! In Jesus' name I pray, Amen.

Write your own short Christmas love letter to Jesus.
Let Him know what Christmas means to you.

If you have not given your life to Jesus but now have decided to turn away from your sin pray this prayer today:

Give Me Five for Fangs, Feathers, and Faith!

Lord Jesus, thank you that you died on the cross for me so long ago. Thank you for forgiving all the sin I have ever done or will do. I am sorry for all the sin I have done in my life. I choose to give you my heart and live for you forever. I accept your free gift of saving grace and thank you for the faith I now have in you. Thank you for hearing my prayer. In Jesus' name I pray, Amen

Bibliography

Tiny but Mighty Fox
  1 Arctic Fox: *Groiler Wildlife Adventure Cards,* Groiler
    Books, Danbury, CN, 1992 (arctic Fox)
  2 Denver Zoo: Arctic Fox: http://www.
    denverzoo.org/animals/arcticFox.asp
  3 Arctic Fox: http://www.zoo.org/animal-facts/arctic-fox

A Whale of A Mammal
  1 Bartoli, Sefania and Boitani, Luigi, *Simon & Schuster's Mammals,*
    Simon & Schuster Inc., New York, NY 1982 page 237
  2 Biggest Mammal: http://www.extremescience.
    com/blue-whale.htm
  3 Blue Whale: http://en.wikipedia.org/wiki/Bluewhale
  4 Biggest Mammal: http://www.extremescience.
    com/blue-whale.htm

Canada's Dall Sheep
  1 Dall Sheep: National Geographic Society, Wild
    Animals of North America, National Geographic
    Society, Washington, DC, 1987 pages 358–359
  2 Dall Sheep: http://library.thinkquest.org/3500/dall_sheep.html
  3 Dall Sheep: http://library.thinkquest
  4 Dall Sheep: National Geographic Society,
    Wild Animals of North America

5 ADF&G Dall Sheep: http://secure.wildlife.
    alaska.gov/index.cfm?adfg=funfacts.sheep
6 ADF&G Dall Sheep: http://secure.wildlife.alaska
7 ADF&G Dall Sheep: http://secure.wildlife.alaska

Waiting on God
1 Seeds; Monocots and Dicots: http://library.
    thinkquest.org/3715/root2.html
2 Some Plants Have Seeds: Reader' Digest Staff, ABC's of
    Nature (A Family Answer Book) Readers Digest Assoc.,
    Pleasantville, New York 1984 pages 88–89 & 98–99
3 Some Plants Have Seeds: Reader' Digest Staff, ABC's of Nature
4 The Power of Seeds: http://www.sproutpeople.
    com/kids/seedpower.print.html

The Marsupial's Marsupium
1 Reader's Digest Staff, Reader's Digest: ABC's of Nature
    (A Family Answer Book), The Reader's Digest Assoc.,
    Inc. Pleasantville, NY, 1984 pages 238–239
2 Marsupial: http://www.academickids.com/
    encyclopedia/index.php/Marsupial
3 The Open Door, The Marsupials: http://www.
    saburchill.com/chapters/chap0038.html
4 Mammals, Marsupials: http://sandiegozoo.
    org/animalbytes/t-marsupial.html
5 Interesting Facts About Marsupials: http://www.bukisa.
    com/articles/61818_interesting-facts-about-marsupials

Caribou Need One Another
1 Arctic Refuge, Caribou: http://arctic.fws.gov/caribou.htm
2 Caribou: http://www.animalcorner.co.uk/wildlife/caribou.html
3 http://www.biokids.umich.edu/critters/Rangifer_tarandus/
4 Caribou: http://www.animalcorner.

Icebergs: God's Life-Supports

1 Icebergs, Just the Facts: http://canadiangeographic.
  ca/magazine/ma06/indepth/justthefacts.asp

2 Climate, Polar Bears: http://wunderground.
  com/climate/PolarBears.asp

3 High Impact Science in Antarctica: J Craig Venter
  Inst: http://blogs.jcvi.org/tag/phytoplankton/

4 All Kinds of Diatoms: http://icestories.exploratorium.
  edu/dispatches/all-kinds-of-diatoms/

Where Eagles Soar

1 Bodo: Norway: http://www.flysas.com/en/
  us/Destinations/Bodo/?vst=true

2 White-tailed sea eagle: http://www.bbc.co.uk/news/10420505

3 Sea Eagle Chicks land in East Scotland: http://www.
  bbc.co.uk/nature/wildfacts/factfiles/208.shtml

4 Bodo: Norway: http://www.flysas.com

5 Soar With Eagles: http://confidenceandjoy.
  com/soar-with-the-eagles/

6.Soar With Eagles: http://confidenceandjoy

Trees Chill Too!

1 Autumn Leaf Color: http://www.
  sciencemadesimple.com/leaves.html

2 Woodworkers Resource: http://www.woodworkersresource.
  com/content/identifing_coniferous_vs_
  deciduous_trees_by_looking_at_leaves/

3 Autumn Leaf Color: http://www.sciencemadesimple.

4 The Life Cycle of the Tree: http://www.myclassifiedcentral.
  com/Article_32240_TheLifeCycleoftheTree.aspx

The Silent Hunter

1 Snowy Owl: http://www.biokids.umich.
   edu/critters/Nyctea_scandiaca/
2 Burton, Robert, Bird Behavior, Alfred A.
   Knopf, New York, NY, 1995, pg. 48

Lake Vostok

1 Observing Weather at the Bottom of the World: http://
   www.weatherwise.org/Archives/Back%20Issues/2010/
   September-October%202010/weather-observing-full.html
2 Lake Vostok Drilling in Antarctica 'running out of time':
   http://www.bbc.co.uk/news/science-environment-12275979
3 Russians Close to Reaching Lake Vostok: http://sptimes.
   ru/index.php?action_id=100&story_id=30838

Butterfly

1Butterfly Life Cycle: http://thebutterflysite.com/facts.shtml
2 Time Frame and Process of a Butterfly: http://
   www.ehow.com/print/how-does_5199747_time-
   process-butterfly-emerging-cocoon.html
3 Butterfly Life Cycle: http://thebutterflysite

The Milky Way = God's Canvas

1 Reader's Digest Staff, Reader's Digest: ABC's of
   Nature (A Family Answer Book), The Reader's Digest
   Assoc., Inc. Pleasantville, NY, 1984 pages 10–11
2 What Are Messier and Other Objects?: http://spacetoday.org/
   DeepSpace/Stars/MessierObjects/MessierObjects.html
3 Reader's Digest Staff, Reader's Digest:
4 The Stars of the Milky Way: http://chview.
   nova.org/chview/chv5.html
5 If the Milky Way: http://www.ucg.org/science/if-milky-way/
6 Star Child Question of the Month http://starchild.gsfc.
   nasa.gov/docs/StarChild/questions/question19.html
7 How Long Will It Take to Travel.... : http://wiki.answers.

com/Q/How_long_would_it_take_to_travel_from_
one_side_of_the_milky way_to_the_other.html

The Donkey—Jesus's Choice

1 The Robinson Ranch (What Can A Donkey Do?): http://www.donkeys.com/inf02.htm (The Robinson Ranch, Madisonville, TX)

2 Reflections on Jesus and the Donkey: http://all-creation.franciscan-anglican.com/donkey.htm

3 ChristStory Bestiary: http:/users.netnitco.net/~legend01/donkey.htm

House of Shell

1 Zim, Herbert S., Smith, Hobart M., Reptiles and Amphibians, Golden Press, New York, NY, 1987 pages 18–19

2 Kids Questions About Turtles: http://www.turtlepuddle.org/kidspage/questions.html

Life Begins in the Egg

1 Burnie, David, *BIRD Eyewitness Books,* Alfred A Knoph, New York 1988 pages 54

2 Egg Biology: http://scienceray.com/biology/science-fact-single-cell-can-be-seen-without-microscope/

3 Eggshells: http://www.absoluteastronomy.com/topics/eggshell

4 Science Project: Egg Strength: http://ezinearticles.com/?Science-Project-for-Kids-To-Show-Egg-Strength&id=921527

5 The Miracle In the Cell: http://www.harunyahya.com/books/science/miracle_in_cell/miracle_cell_09.php

The Oyster's Secret

1 Pearl: en.wikipedia.org/wiki/Oyster_pearl

2 How Do Oysters Make Pearls?: http://www.ehow.com/how-does_5474558_do-oysters-make-pearls.html

3 Pearl: en.wikipedia.org/

4 How Do Oysters Make Pearls?: http://

Big Harry!
1 Goliath Bird-Eating Spider: http://www.blueplanetbiomes.
   org/goliath_bird_eating_spider.htm
2 What's Huge, Harry, and Has Fangs… : http://
   nationalzoo.si.edu/Animals/Invertebrates/Facts/
   FactSheets/GoliathBirdEatingTarantula.cfm
3 Goliath Bird-Eating Spider: http://www.blueplanetbiomes.org
4 Goliath Bird-Eating Spider: http://www.blueplanetbiomes
5 Biggest Spider: http://www.extremescience.
   com/biggest-spider.htm
6 Goliath Bird-Eating: http://www.blueplanetbiomes.
7 Mound, Lawrence, and Brooks, Stephen, Insects, Dorling
   Kindersley, London, New York, 1995, page 107.
8 Goliath Bird: http://www.blueplanetbiomes.

Tools for Success
1 American Kestrel: http://www.allaboutbirds.
   org/guide/American_Kestrel/lifehistory
2 American Kestrel: http://www.allaboutbirds.org/guide
3 Burton, Robert, *Bird Behavior,* Alfred A.
   Knopf, New York, NY, 1995 pages 103
4 What Is An American Kestrel: http://encycl.
   opentopia.com/term/American_Kestrel
5 American Kestrel: http://www.birdinginformation.
   com/birds/falcons-and-kites/american-kestrel/

Giraffes Come in One Size
1 Gerstenfeld, Sheldon L., Zoo Clues: Making The
   Most of Your Visit to the Zoo, Viking; Penguin
   Group, New York, NY pages 60–62
2 Gerstenfeld, Sheldon L., Zoo Clues:
3 The Giraffe: Green, Victoria, Nature Friend
   Magazine, December 1996 pages 14–15
4 The Giraffe: Green, Victoria, Nature Friend
5 Gerstenfeld, Sheldon L
6 Giraffe: www.sandiegozoo.org/animalbytes/t-giraffe.html

God's Jackhammer

1 15 Fun Facts About Woodpeckers: http://birding.about.com/
   od/birdprofiles/a/15-Fun-Facts-About-Woodpeckers.htm?p=1
2 The Marvel of God's Creation: http://www.present-truth.org/3-
   Nature/Evolution%20of%20Creationist/MOGC%2010.htm
3 15 Fun Facts About Woodpeckers: http://birding.about.com/
   od/birdprofiles/a/15-Fun-Facts-About-Woodpeckers.htm?p=1
4 Woodpeckers: http://www.defenders.org/wildlife_
   and_habitat/wildlife/woodpeckers.php

Living Together... Buddies

1 Robinson, Michael H. and Challinor, David, Zoo Animals: A
   Smithsonian Guide, Macmillan, New York, NY 1995 page 23
2 Odd Couples: http://magma.nationalgeographic.
   com/ngexplorer/0601/articles/mainarticle.html
3 Parker, Steve, *Fish, Eyewitness Books,* Alfred A.
   Knopf, New York, NY 1990 pages 46–47

Hibernation—God's Great Escape

1 Leokum, Arkady, The Big Book of Tell Me Why, Barnes
   and Noble, New York, NY 1986 Vol. 1 pages 136–137
2 How Hibernation Works: http://animals.howstuffworks.
   com/animal-facts/hibernation.htm/printable
3 How Hibernation Works: http://animals.howstuffworks.com
4 1 Leokum, Arkady, The Big Book of Tell Me Why

Cuckoo Catfish

1 The Cuckoo Catfish: http://indianapublicmedia.
   org/amomentofscience/excuse-baby-mout/
2 Ganeri, Anita, Animals and Their Young,
   Wilton, CT 06897 1994 pg 20–21
3 The Cuckoo Catfish: http://indianapublicmedia.org

The Kitten and the Crow

1 www.youtube.com/watch?v=1JiJzqXxgxo (Titled the Miracle Pet)

Who Is the Center of Your World?

1 Sun: http://www.edu.pe.ca/southernkings/Sun.htm

2 Facts About the Sun: http://www.newsdial.com/
outerspace/facts-about-the-sun.html

3 Speed of Light: http://en.wikipedia.org/wiki/Speed_of_light

4 The Sun: http://library.thinkquest.org/J002741/Sun.htm

5 Sun: http://www.edu.

6 Sun For Kids: http://www.nasa.gov/vision/universe/
solarsystem/sun_for_kids_main.html

7 The Sun: http://library.thinkquest

8 Sun For Kids: http://www.nasa.gov

9 The Sun: http://library.

Where Did All the Bugs Go?

1 Klots, Alexander B. and Elsie B., 1001 Questions
Answered About Insects, Dover Publications,
Inc., New York 1961 pages 118–121

2 Where Do Insects Go In Winter: http://www.si.edu/
Encyclopedia_SI/nmnh/buginfo/winter.htm

3 Where Do Insects Go: http://www.si.edu/

Snow Geese: V= Victory

1 Migrating Geese: http://www.wbu.com/
chipperwoods/photos/geese.htm

2 Fly Like Geese!: http://www.obeosphere.
com/2008/04/fly-like-geese/

3 Migrating Geese: http://www.wbu.com/chipperwoods/

4 Lessons From Geese: http://www.somerton.k12.az.us/geese.html

5 Ornithology: Bird Flight II: http://people.eku.edu/
ritchisong/RITCHISO/554notes3.html

6 Migrating Geese: http://www.wbu.

Northern California Giants

1 Hyperion- World's Tallest Redwood: http://www.mdvaden.com/redwood_hyperion.shtml
2 Sequoia Sempervirens: http://en.wikipedia.org/wiki/Sequoia_sempervirens
3 The Redwood Forest: Water: http://sunnyfortuna.com/explore/redwoods_and_water.htm

High-Tech Ears

1 Williams, Heathcote, *Sacred Elephant,* Harmony Books, New York, NY 1929 pages 106–107
2 Infrasound: en.wikipedia.org/wiki/Infrasound

Death Valley—Mega Hot!

1 Death Valley: http://www.yellowecho.com/travel/death_valley_facts.htm
2 Surviving Summer in Death Valley: http://www.desertusa.com/mag98/june/stores/dvheat.html
3 Crotalus Cerastes: http://en.wikipedia.org/wiki/Crotalus_cerastes

The Camel—God's Desert Taxi

1 Gerstenfeld, Sheldon L., Zoo Clues: Making the Most of Your Visit to the Zoo, Viking, Published by Penguin Group, New York, NY 1991 pages 56–59
2 All About Camels: http://www.marisamontes.com/all_about_camels.htm
3 Dromedary Camel: http://www.windyhillranch.com/camel.htm
4 Gerstenfeld, Sheldon L., *Zoo* Clues:

Equator = Weather 24/7 Same!Forcast: Humid and Hot

1 Equator Countries: http://www.infoplease.com/askeds/countries-equator.html
2 Equator: http://encyclopedia.kids.net.au/page/eq/Equator

3 Seasons at the Equator: http://wiki.answers.com/Q/
   Why_do_countries_at_the_equator_have_no_seasons
4 Equator: http://encyclopedia.kids.net.au/page/eq/Equator

Nature's Clean-Up Crew
1 Dung Beetles: http://static.test.hq.nationalgeographic.com/
   wpf/sites/kids/NGS/wpf/printcreature/dung-beetle.html
2 Dung Beetle Facts: http://www.kidscantravel.
   com/familyvacationdestinations/falsebaypark/
   funstuffkids/index.html
3 Insects: Dung Beetle: http://www.sandiegozoo.
   org/animalbytes/t-dung_beetle.html

Bats Get A Bad Rap
1 Graham, Gary L., *Bats of the World,* Western Publishing
   Co. Inc., Racine, WI 1994 pages 4–49
2 Swartz Lab: http://www.brown.edu/Departments/
   EEB/EML/background/bat_basics.htm
3 Graham, Gary L., *Bats of the World,*
4 All About Bats: www.batcon.org
5 E Newsletter Archive: http://www.batcon.org/index.php/
   component/mailing/?task=_viewArticle&ArticleID=1125

Two Are Better Than One
1 Insects: http://www.biokids.umich.edu/critters/Insecta/
2 Termite: http://en.wikipedia.org/wiki/Insect
3 Termites: http://www.biokids.umich.edu/critters/Isoptera/
4 Termites: http://www.biokids.
5 What Do Termites Mounds Look like: http://www.ehow.
   com/about_4587093_do-termite-mounds-look-like.html

Big Bubba
1 Polar Bears: http://www.polarbearsinternational.org/
   sites/default/files/pdf/PolarBearsComprehensive.pdf
2 Robinson, Michael H. and Challinor, David,

Zoo Animals, A Smithsonian Guide, Macmillan, New York, NY 1995 pages 196–197

Tiny Critters with Big Jobs
1 Ten Ways to Bugproof: http://home.howstuffworks. com/home-improvement/household-safety/ tips/10-ways-to-bug-proof-your-home.htm
2 Another Link in Food Chain: http://www. geography4kids.com/files/land_foodchain.html

Thermometers with Wings
1 Ask a Cricket: http://www.sciencebuddies.org/science-fair-projects/project_ideas/Zoo_p055.shtml
2 Chemical Reactions: http://en.wikipedia. org/wiki/Chemical_reaction

God Is the True Light
1 Stars: http://science.nationalgeographic.com/ science/space/universe/stars-article.html
2 Power of Light: http://science.nationalgeographic. com/science/space/universe/power-of-light.html
3 Bible: Genesis 1/John 1

The Oceans Jellies
1 Jellyfish: http://en.wikipedia.org/wiki/Jelly_fish
2 What Are Jellyfish Made of? : http://oceanservice. noaa.gov/facts/oceanfacts.php
3 Jellyfish: http://library.thinkquest.org/CR0215242/jellyfish.htm
4 Scyphozoa: More on Morphology: http://www.ucmp. berkeley.edu/cnidaria/scyphozoamm.html
5 Jellyfish: http://en.wikipedia
6 Jellyfish Species: http://www.jellyfishfacts. net/jellyfish-species.html

Tiny Titans

1 Fire Ant Information: http://www.fireant.net/
2 Basic Information: http://www.controlfireants.com/overview.htm
3 Red Imported Fireants: http://buginfo.com/article.cfm?id=11
4 Red Imported: http://buginfo.com/

What Was That? .A Bird or a Bee

1 http://birdfreak.com/review-hummingbirds-of-north-america/
2 http://www.buzzle.com/articles/facts-about-the-hummingbirds.html
3 http://www.buzzle.com/articles/facts-about-the-hummingbirds.html
4 http://www.experiencefestival.com/a/Bee_Hummingbird/id/1929550
5 http://www.avianweb.com/beehummingbirds.html

Aphid Lions

1 How Does a Ladybug Fly?: http://www.ehow.com/how-does_4609983_a-ladybug-fly.html
2 Insect: Beetle: http://insect-beetle.info/index.html
3 Ladybugs: http://animals.nationalgeographic.com/animals/bugs/ladybug/
4 Largest Group of Animals: http://answers.yahoo.com/question/index?qid=20081125093401AA2DmXS
5 Ladybug, Ladybug: http://www.sherriallen.com/garden/ladybugs.html
6 Ladybug, Ladybug: http://www.sherriallen.
7 Do Ladybugs protect plants?: http://insect-beetle.info/index.html
8 Ladybug Skeleton: wiki.answers.com/Q/Do_ladybugs_have_exoskeletons

God's Masterpieces

1 Photos Show Its True: No Two Snowflakes Alike: http://www.livescience.com/546-photos-show-true-snowflakes-alike.html

2 How Snowflakes Are Formed: http://factoidz.
  com/how-snowflakes-are-formed/
3 How Snowflakes Are Formed: "factoids"
4 How Snowflakes Are Formed: "factoids"
5 Snowflake Chemistry: http://chemistry.about.com/
  od/moleculescompounds/a/snowflake.htm?p=1

Dumbo Octopus
1 Dumbo Octopus: http://ww.hubpages.
  com/hub/Dumbo-Octopus
2 Challenger Deep: http://www.kids-fun-
  science.com/challenger-deep.html

Venus Flytrap
1 Reader' Digest Staff, *ABC's of Nature (A Family Answer Book)*
  Readers Digest Assoc., Pleasantville, New York 1984 page 117

Hot Dogs with an Attitude
1 The Naked Truth about Mole Rats: http://nationalzoo.
  si.edu/Publications/ZooGoer/2002/3/nakedmolerats.cfm

The Big and Mighty Amazon
1 Amazon River: http://geography.about.com/od/
  specificplacesofinterest/a/amazonriver8.htm
2 World's Greatest River: http://www.
  extremescience.com/amazon-river.htm
3 World's Greatest River: http://www.extremescience
4 World's Greatest River: http://www.extremescience
5 Nasa: Amazon River:
http://www.nasaimages.org/luna/servlet/view/search?Quic
  kSearchA=QuickSearchA&q=sts-43+amazon+river+
6 nationalzoo.si.edu/Animals/Amazonia/Facts/basinfacts.cfm

Nothing is Hidden from God

1 Seahorses: http://ani http://www.nwf.org/Kids/
Ranger-2 Rick/Animals/Fish/Seahorses.aspxmals.
nationalgeographic.com/animals/fish/sea-horse.html

2 Seahorses: http://www.ehow.com/
info_8569195_seahorse-kids.html

3 Seahorses: http://ani http://www.nwf.org/Kids/Ranger

Blink, Blink, Blink Bugs

1 Firefly: http://animals.nationalgeographic.
com/animals/bugs/firefly.html

2 Fireflies Blink in Sync: http://www.sciencedaily.
com/releases/2010/07/100708141539.htm

3 Firefly: http://animals.nationalgeographic

We Are the Sheep of His Pasteur

1 Keller, W Phillip, A Shepherd Looks At Psalm
23, Zondervan, Grand Rapids MI, 1970

Conversion Chart for all measurements;

http://www.sciencemadesimple.com/length_conversion.php